Embracing Me

Yasmine Brown

EMBRACING ME

Copyright © 2022 Yasmine Brown

All rights reserved. No portion of this book may be reproduced, stored in a retrieval system, or transmitted in any form or by any means; electronic, mechanical, photocopy, recording, scanning, or other, except for brief quotations in critical reviews or articles, without the prior written permission of the author.

Cover design by Yasmine Brown

Literary consulting, developmental editing, and formatting, by Clara Rose & Company.

Published by RoseDale Publishing
12100 Cobble Stone Drive, Suite 3
Bayonet Point, Florida 34667

ISBN-13: 979-8-9859515-4-7

RoseDale
Publishing

EMBRACING ME

EMBRACING ME

FOREWORD

It has been a pleasure to pastor Yasmine Brown and her family for the past 3 years. We met when she volunteered to help with one of our church's outreaches. From the first day we met I admired her love for the community and the people she shared the gospel with. She and her family have been faithful members, serving in many capacities, within the church. Yasmine's passion to help women pursue their call is admirable and her zeal for God is contagious.

Her new book, *Embracing Me*, is a delightful read. Yasmine's sincere, honest, and upfront approach keeps you glued to the pages. When you read about her personal journey, and the process she went through to fulfill the plan God had for her, you will be inspired to take steps towards your own purpose.

Get ready to be stirred up to make moves towards your goals. This is a must read and it is an honor to have been one of the first to read it.

Pastor Clover Williams

The River Church at Fort Myers

EMBRACING ME

DEDICATION

This book is dedicated to my husband, Fabian.
You have been extremely instrumental throughout my entire transformation. You hung in there with me, literally for the better or worse, in sickness, and in health.

The nights I cried because I felt like I was not good enough, you encouraged me and said I was more than enough.

The times I was sick and didn't think I would make it through the night, you prayed for healing over my mind and body, by speaking the word of God over my life.

When I was afraid of taking on the task that came along with my calling to serve, you would always say, "Shorty, you got this!"

You are my biggest supporter and I love you for that. I am the happiest woman today because you love all of me, and you allow me to be who God called me to be.

To my daughter Aryonna, my precious firstborn.
You taught me how to be your first example of a strong Black woman in your life. I am so proud to be your mom. You are my bright happy sunshine. God

has great plans for your life because your steps are ordered by Him.

To my son, Stephen who is my heartbeat.
Your adventurous spirit has taught me not to fret. I take pride in being your mom, you are an extraordinary young man and God also has great plans for your life. You were predestined to be great from the beginning.

You both are my legacy.

TABLE OF CONTENTS

FOREWORD 5

DEDICATION 7

ACKNOWLEDGMENTS 11

PREFACE 13

Step 1: Your Identity.. 17

   Who am I 19

Step 2: Owner's manual 31

   Seeking Your Creator 33

   Seeking Your Purpose 43

   Believing in Prayer 61

Step 3: Resetting You 79

   Transforming Your Mind....................................... 81

Step 4: The Liberty.. 99

   Walking in Power 101

   Walking in Love.. 113

   Walking in Soundness 125

Step 5: Accepting You 133

   Embracing Your Gift 135

   Embracing Me... 151

About the AUTHOR.. 163

EMBRACING ME

ACKNOWLEDGMENTS

I stand on the shoulders of many people who have played a significant role in my life, whether it be momentarily or for long periods of time. I'd like to recognize and thank them here.

Thank you to my husband who always believed in me. His words of encouragement always gave me the hope to go forth, no matter what.

Thank you to my mommy who calls me and checks up on me to see how I'm doing. She always says, *You are okay, you fine, you strong baby.*

Thank you to my daughter, son, team, and staff who help me keep everything together by doing what they are great at, so that I can focus on doing what I was called to do.

Thank you to my family and friends who are always ready to support and serve whenever I need them.

Thank you to my leaders, pastors, mentors, and coaches who prayed for me, encouraged, and equipped me with what I needed to go forth in this journey.

Thank you to Elonza Morris, III for helping me put the book outline together and who told me my story needed to be heard.

Thank you to my consultant and publisher for taking my late-night calls and responding to my emails and text messages, weird hours of the day lol. She helped me craft my message for the world.

Many Thanks,

Yasmine Brown

PREFACE

First and foremost, I thank God for inspiring me to write this book. Since God is the author and the finisher of my faith, why not give Him thanks for giving me the ability to be an author? I'm reminded of the scripture Psalms 45:1 which says:

> *"My heart is overflowing with a good matter; I speak of things which I have made touching the king. My tongue is the pen of a ready writer."*

You see, I can appreciate who God has made me into today because I know who I was, where I came from, what I experienced, and how the Holy Spirit transformed my life. I decided to share my story because people often see the glory of God in the life of another, but they don't really know what that person went through to get to where they are. This chronicles my journey of transformation.

It started when I found myself seeking God and asking; *Who am I and what is your purpose for this life you have given to me?* I wanted more because it felt like there was more to life. It was like something was nudging me on the inside to *keep asking and you'll receive, keep seeking and you shall find, and knocking and the door will open*. Honestly, I really did not know what it was, I just knew there was something greater.

As time went on, I developed a relationship with the Holy Spirit. I had a hunger for the word of God, and I was hungry and thirsty for more.

> *"Blessed are they which do hunger and thirst after righteousness; for they shall be filled."*
> *Matthew 5:6*

The more He filled me, the more I wanted and the more I desired to please Him, because I was so in love with Him. I wanted to live for Him. This is where I believe my quest began. I needed to find God's will for my life.

It is my prayer that, as you read this book, you will receive a revelation and knowledge of what God's plans are for your life and, as the Holy Spirit leads you, you will embrace it.

I love the Amplified version of the Bible, which gives us simple instructions for how to go through this process, so we can live a fulfilled life and not just exist.

> *"Ask and keep on asking and it will be given to you; seek and keep on seeking and you will find; knock and keep on knocking and the door will be opened to you. For everyone who keeps on asking receives, and he who keeps on seeking finds, and to him who keeps on*

knocking, it will be opened." Matthew 7:7-8

It is my hope you will be liberated and experience the same freedom I have. It is life changing. It was an eye-opening experience, the moment I accepted who I was and who God created me to be.

I began to grow and blossom into the beautiful person you see today. I had this radiating smile that glowed. My confidence in Him soared because I knew who I was. My mental, spiritual, and physical senses were sparked, and I was renewed and transformed. It felt like I was catapulted into another dimension. The experience was mind-blowing.

The transformation is a process, so be patient with yourself. Some things will happen miraculously in an instant. Others may happen progressively over time.

In this book, you will learn the 5 key things that helped me on this journey:

1. Finding my identity
2. Reading my owner's manual
3. Hitting the restart button
4. Walking in liberty
5. Accepting who I was created to be

I call it a journey because it did not happen overnight for me. It was indeed a process, but worth every moment.

EMBRACING ME

Awakening Your Gift

STEP 1: YOUR IDENTITY

EMBRACING ME

CHAPTER 1
Who am I

Who am I? This is the number one question every living soul asks, at one point or another in their life. This is the big question that can become frustrating, because there are so many things that can mislead us. Especially with all the distractions the world throws at us.

We look at other people's lives and we try to fashion our own lives after them. What are you doing? *That* is not your life, or the plan God has for you. That is their life.

We see images, icons, brands, celebrities, billboards, media, and sometimes even our friends and family, doing things we admire. All these things and people, which we may idolize and worship, or want to be like, are false images of our own self-perception.

There is nothing wrong with admiring someone or gleaning from them. It's okay to have a role model, mentor, or someone you really look up to. However, there is a problem when you say or think you are that person.

With all the billions of people walking on the face of

this earth, none are alike. Not even twins. Every single last one of us is unique. There is only one YOU, but finding out who you really are, is a journey.

I grew up in a loving yet hostile environment. I was born and raised in a neighborhood of Miami, called Little Haiti. During the late 1980's and early 1990's, there were many gang-related activities going on in our neighborhood. There was rivalry over territories and holding down their turf. You had the Haitians, the Americans, the Puerto Ricans, the Cubans, and the Haitian African Americans, all jockeying for position and control. It was all nonsense.

I was caught in between two worlds, being born in the US, and being born to Haitian parents, but I identified myself as a Haitian girl and not an American.

Although I was not attacked personally, many Haitian immigrants were. Even at a very young age, I knew this was stupid and ignorant. I could not stomach it when people were being ostracized, beaten, and humiliated because of their race, color, or where they were from. I mean, who does that? To me, this was the epitome of ignorance!

Haitians were being beaten by the African Americans

as though they were not human beings, simply because they were foreigners. It was the worst thing you can imagine seeing growing up. I found myself fighting and forced to choose a side. Not because I was being targeted, but because I chose to stand up for those who had no one to stand up for them.

This conflict created an environment where I either had to fight or flee. Some might have kept their mouths shut or looked the other way out of fear. Some felt like it isn't any of their business. Let's just say I was different. For some reason, fear was never a thought for me. What was happening was wrong and something had to be done about it.

I identified with Haitians because I grew up in Little Haiti and in a Haitian household with Haitian culture. I only spoke one language as a child before going to school, Creole. English was my second language. Thank God for ESOL (English for Speakers of Other Languages).

Having ten siblings, we were taught by our parents to always stick together no matter what. Since I identified as Haitian, siding with the Haitian immigrants was a no brainer. But this often created an awkward position for me, since I didn't choose my friends based on where they came from. I befriended anyone. It did not matter to me.

Funny how they saw no difference between me and them, yet they saw a difference between the "Haitian immigrants" we called islanders, and themselves. Nevertheless, I saw them as enemies and felt like I had to protect my own. I fell into the same trap.

Growing up, I attended a magnet school outside of my zone because my parents thought it would be safer. Our middle school, *El Portel*, was in a middle-class prestigious neighborhood across the bridge from the Largmont projects. Instead of walking all the way around the community to catch the metro bus home, we would take a shortcut across *the bridge*.

Many of the fights we had, when crossing the bridge or on the public bus, were atrocious. Every day, right before school ended, anxiety and stress levels were high, because you did not know what was going to happen. It could be a good day, or it could be a bad day, we never knew what to expect.

On a good day, a group of us would stop by the candy lady's house to buy frozen cups, chips, and pickled eggs with hot sausage, as we laughed and walked to the bus station.

On a bad day, we ran to see what the commotion was down the street from the school, because a fight had just broken out.

I was often told this was not my fight, or this had nothing to do with me and I should stay out of it. My reply was always, "No! I will not stand by and watch you beat and jump on a person because they are a Haitian immigrant! You must come through me!" Usually, these fights broke out suddenly, and without saying a word, I would just jump in to rescue someone. Of course, I ended up swinging and throwing jabs, landing blows anywhere I could.

Imagine dealing with this on the outside and having to deal with the Haitian culture at home, where domestic violence was acceptable.

I was traumatized as a child. As time went on and I witnessed it repeatedly, I became numb, confused, angry, and resentful. I became a ticking time bomb and a fighting machine, full of hate, aggression, defiance and unforgiveness. I mimicked what I hated. As a result, I fought bullies and anyone who picked on people they knew were no match for them. I looked for someone to release all my anger and frustration on. I did not care who it was. If you gave me a reason, I was fighting somebody that day. I can't tell you a corner I did not fight on.

I was walking in the spirit of rage, always ready to explode on anyone who gave me an opportunity. Fighting was therapeutic for me, it felt good. I know that sounds sick, but I was, the rage was gratifying and soothing to me. No one knew it because in our culture we don't believe in seeing therapist or psychiatric doctor.

They called me *She-Ra* and I believed *this was who I was*. I was the Haitian girl on the block that was a force to be reckoned with. I was known as the bad, quick tempered, feisty girl. The girl who would beat a person to a pulp or until she saw blood, then go on her way like nothing happened. The girl who would spazz out and go from 0 to 10,000 in a split second. The female version of the Incredible Hulk, they said.

Some days, I wanted to control my temper, but I just couldn't. I'd get super-hot, my ears would burn, my heart would palpitate really fast, and then I'd black out. Most of the time whatever transpired during those black outs, I could never recall. It felt like something took over me.

One time I was braiding a client's hair in our backyard, and I heard a young lady was calling my name out about some foolishness. We were already beefing. I politely told the client I would be back. I ran upstairs. I changed into biker shorts with a tank top. Then I tucked my hair into a tight ponytail. In my mind, I was saying, I am going to settle this once and for all.

I walked about 2 blocks with my siblings and friends to her house. I called her outside, yelling at the top of my lungs, "Hey, come outside!" She stood at the door talking to me, so I walked up to the door, snatched it open, and pulled her out of the house. I snapped and blacked out.

I only stopped because I heard the police siren and my siblings and friends yelling, "Yasmine stop you have blood on you. Stop 5-O, are coming." They eventually pulled me off her and separated us. I ran back home, I changed my clothes, and went back to doing my clients braids as though nothing had happened.

People would ask me about the fights, and I honestly would not remember them. This was all I knew. I was a little girl trapped in the body of a teen, who would eventually become an angry adult. If you crossed me, you were going to catch these hands, PERIOD!

Not realizing this was a false identity of mine, I had adapted to my environment, thinking this was who I was. My identity was hidden, and I had no clue of who I really was outside of my environment. If someone asked me who I was then, I would not have an answer because I did not have a clue, let alone know what that even meant.

In my journey, I had to go through a process of *Detoxification of Identity*™. I had to go through the process of peeling away all the toxic substances, false concepts, character traits, and bad habits I had picked up through the course of my life. I identified with them, but they were not who I was.

I am so grateful the Holy Spirit opened my eyes to what I needed. Some people go through treatment to detox from drugs or alcohol, I needed to have a complete inner-man detox.

I literally went through a process of transformation, as I was purged from toxic thinking, talking, acting, perception and living. At one point, it felt like I was losing my mind; I was so torn between what I was comfortable with and the new inner voice guiding me, that I would just cry.

What seemed normal for some people, was abnormal for me. As a new person in Christ, I had to learn a NEW normal. Of course, this is subjective; cultural background and how you are raised play a significant part in your make up as a person. But I was being transformed as God was renewing my mind!

Take a moment to evaluate yourself. Remember, you are not your environment or your situation, and your circumstance is not your identity. Who are you apart from that? Are you living with a false identity? Give yourself time to let that question sink in and process it. I want you to discover the real you.

It's time to ask yourself some questions. "Who are you at your core?" What does it look like? Are you confident and happy with your responses, and proud of who you are? How does it make you feel? Be completely honest with yourself.

Are there some things you want to change about yourself? I'm not talking about cosmetic things, there is nothing wrong with that, but I'm talking about your inner man. The true YOU. The person you are when no one is watching.

We are forever learning and constantly making

improvements, to reach our greatest potential and be the best version of who we were created to be.

If you think you're good, will you allow room for growth? Perhaps, you may consider going through the process of detoxification. This is a process. Are you ready for a change? Are you ready to be the person you were created to be?

Awakening Your Gift

REFLECTION JOURNALING

Take a notebook and begin writing down what comes to your mind when you ask yourself the following question(s). Be completely honest with yourself.

- Who am I at my core?
- What does it look like?

Are you confident and happy with your responses, and proud of who you are? How does it make you feel?

EMBRACING ME

Awakening Your Gift

STEP 2: OWNER'S MANUAL

EMBRACING ME

CHAPTER 2
Seeking Your Creator

Right before I graduated from high school, someone witnessed to me. He shared that God loved me and had a plan for my life, and he invited me to church. When I walked into the service, the environment was different. Not the traditional Catholic church service I was used to. The man preaching captivated me, and his words pierced my heart, and I started crying uncontrollably. It was the word of God that transformed my life.

I will never forget it. He asked me to come forward, he led me to Christ with the sinner's prayer. I repeated this verse after him: Romans 10:9-10

> *9) That if thou shalt confess with thy mouth the Lord Jesus, and shalt believe in thine heart that God hath raised him from the dead, thou shalt be saved. 10) For with the heart man believeth unto righteousness; and with the mouth confession is made unto salvation.*

As he laid his hands on me and prayed, my knees buckled. On my knees sobbing and crying, because I felt so free and relieved, it felt like a soft electrical current was running throughout my entire body. It was what I'd been looking for, and my life was never the same after April 1997. I felt like I was a new person, but I had no idea who I was yet.

After receiving Jesus and accepting Him as my Lord and personal savior, I started developing a relationship with God. I had a lot of questions for Him. "Why am I here? What am I supposed to do with my life? Who am I? Lord, can you please help me out?" Having no idea how he would respond, or what he might do, I waited on Him.

Our true identity is not in what we think it is. Sometimes we associate ourselves with where we came from or what we've gone through, or even what our current situation is now, but that is far from the truth. Those things do not dictate who we really are. I could not change where I came from, who my parents were, or what circumstance or situations I found myself in. It didn't matter because that did not define who I was or determine my final destination.

In our search for truth, we read, listen to, and watch anything we think can tell us… who we are or what our purpose is. Yet as believers we already have access to the truth, if we will only ask.

The Bible tells us to ask God!

> *"If any of you lack wisdom, let him ask of God, that giveth to all men liberally, and upbraideth not; and it shall be given him."*
>
> *"But let him ask in faith, nothing wavering. For he that wavereth is like a wave of the sea driven with the wind tossed." James 1:5*

At first, I was wavering in what I was asking for, and as a result, I went through life's difficulties. I didn't understand that, whatever I had sought God for, I was supposed to receive it by faith. Then, after I had suffered and gone through enough of the rocky, bumpy roads of life, it came to me; there must be a greater plan in life than this.

The Holy Spirit was there to direct me the entire time but sometimes we allow what people say, our worries, and our distractions of what's going on around us, to deter us from what our soul truly yearns for.

When I eventually asked God for help, He was pointing me in the right direction. But I then sought men to validate what God had already instructed me to do, simply because I had more faith in man than God. It was early in my spiritual walk, and I did not yet believe the Holy Spirit would lead and guide me into all truth.

Over time, as my relationship with God grew, I came to discover that we have the answers at our fingertips. For the most part, there are instructions to everything in life. Most instructions come in the form of an owner's manual. Indeed, we do have an owner's manual for this life.

When I think of an owner's manual, I think of a product such as a vehicle, exercise equipment, or a cell phone. All of which have owner's manuals that come packaged with the products or can be downloaded off the manufacturer's website.

To understand how a product works and get the most utilization from it, one should consider reading the owner's manual, right? Yet most of us bypass the manual. We go straight to the product and figure how it operates by ourselves. At least we try to.

Somehow, we figure it is probably common sense, but if we get stuck, we can always look for the answer in the owner's manual or call customer service. We usually don't even attempt to see what the designer of the product tells us to do with it or how to use it unless we get frustrated because something isn't working properly. All of which would not be as complicated if we would simply read the owner's manual. In my opinion, we could avoid a lot of mishaps if we'd learn to pick up the owner's manual and READ IT.

We own a new 2021 Chevy Tahoe Truck. We automatically assumed that premium gas would be better because it's a premium truck, right? That was far from the truth. After going through the owner's manual, a few months later, we discovered the Tahoe performs better with regular gas. Can you imagine how much money we spent unnecessarily, simply because we didn't know better, since we didn't bother to read the owner's manual?

There is a bogus saying, "What you don't know won't hurt you." This is not true. What you don't know can harm you or have an adverse effect on you. Being ignorant does not save you from calamity. If you didn't know a red light meant *stop*, and you ran through one, you could get injured or possibly lose your life or cause harm to someone else. It is good, even necessary, to *be knowledgeable* about things, especially concerning the safety of your life.

Similarly, it is good to know which gas and oil will give you the most usage, more mileage, and help the car perform better.

Years ago, we had a 2008 Buick Lacrosse. At the time I did not know the transmission fluid was supposed to be changed after so many miles. We did the regular oil maintenance, tire rotation, etc., but we're clueless about the transmission service.

As a result, the transmission blew. The car was disabled and could not be driven unless we replaced the transmission. At the time we did not have the extra funds to purchase another transmission.

It would be easy to blame those who serviced the car for me at the time, but what difference would that make? It was my vehicle, and it was my responsibility to make sure it got properly serviced.

Both mistakes were costly. The point is, all of this could have been avoided had we educated ourselves, by simply reading the owner's manual.

What if I told you that you don't need to lose a car to learn that regular maintenance will keep it running longer?

What If I told you there is a better way to do things and you do not necessarily have to learn the hard way? You could actually learn without the hard knocks of life.

Although some of my experiences helped me become a better person and mold who I am today; if I could have learned some things prior or learned from someone else's mistakes, I would be a lot further today.

Some mistakes are costly. Heck, some mistakes can cost you your life. No one wants that. Unfortunately, most mistakes cause some sort of setback. Who wants to learn that way?

Of course, as humans we do make mistakes, it allows us the room to grow gracefully into better people. We should be proactively seeking the one who knows every fiber of our being, down to the strands of hair on our heads. It is in seeking our creator and reading the owner's manual that we can live the highest and best version of what He created us to be.

Now that you know you can seek your creator about your life, take a few minutes to jot down some questions you want to ask Him. He is always available to you.

I'll share what I practice, to give you a starting point. First, I find a private place. Then I quiet my mind and remove all distractions. I center myself in Him and invite His presence by simply thanking Him. Yes, just me and my creator (GOD). I start meditating on positive things, such as thanking Him for LOVE.

My mind may try to wonder elsewhere with another thought, but I calmly redirect my thoughts again, saying *thank you for LOVE*. Once I get there, in His presence, I speak to Him as I'm speaking to you. I pour out my heart and ask Him whatever question I have. After I am done, I sit still and wait. In waiting for a response, I can hear what He says. It comes from within. Afterward, I thank Him again.

Can you take a few minutes to invite Jesus into your space? You don't have to do it exactly the way I do it, the objective is to get into God's presence, speak to him, and allow Him to minister back to you. Try not to be in a rush when you are doing this. The peace that will come upon you is unexplainable, it is the most gratifying experience.

After you meditate, jot down your experience in your notebook. Start journaling regularly, so you can see your progress. Growth is measurable.

This new journey will change your life forever.

Awakening Your Gift

REFLECTION JOURNALING

Take a notebook and begin writing down what comes to your mind when you ask yourself the following question(s). Be completely honest with yourself.

- When was the last time you sought your creator?
- Sit quietly and seek your creator, then briefly explain what your experience was like.

EMBRACING ME

CHAPTER 3
Seeking Your Purpose

As a teen, I imagined myself becoming a businesswoman. It was clear as day. I had a two-piece pencil skirt suit, with a legal pad and a pen in my hand. That vision was God speaking to me. He gave me a glimpse of what I would be in the future. Yet, that vision was for an appointed time.

Would I be an employee in a business or start my own? I did not understand this vision until I was in my early thirties. I must admit, I did not have a full understanding of who I was or what my purpose was.

> *"Write the vision and engrave it plainly on tablets so that the one who reads it will run." Habakkuk 2:2*

No one was telling me to start my own business back then. My mom was adamant about me going to college and becoming a nurse, a doctor, or a lawyer. That's most Haitian parents' dreams for their children. Whatever they could not become, they tried to live it out vicariously through their children.

Personally, I had no desire for any of those professions, but I went to college because that's what they wanted me to do. I wanted to please them, so I did it for them and not myself. I knew I wanted something more in life.

I watched videos, attended seminars, and attended institutions for answers. Some of which enhanced my knowledge and taught me how to implement certain systems. Yet, they could never answer the question, "What is my purpose?"

Who am I? What is my purpose? When will it happen and how will I get there? These are the big questions we all ask ourselves at some point.

I asked different people, who I thought might have the answers, but they did not. At the time I didn't realize, that was a God question, not one for man.

One of the institutions I registered at was a community college. I could not make up my mind about my future to save my life, and I was hoping to find the answers while attending school. But every semester I was changing my career path. I wondered, *why does it seem like I am living an aimless life? Why does it seem like my colleagues know exactly what they want to major and minor in?*

I tried psychology, but I could not agree with the theories they were teaching at the time, it went against what I believed. You must understand, I was a babe in Christ and did not know how to decipher and navigate both.

Now that I am mature, I can defend my beliefs, get what I need, and then make it my own, in my own practice. Had I known then what I know now, I would have probably responded differently.

Then I tried physical therapy, and then I bounced to criminal justice, and eventually realized I did not like any of them. What was I supposed to do? Here I was in college with no final destination. I knew I wanted to be someone great, I just could not find it in their list of careers.

What I discovered was; you don't have to be on the list. Perhaps the reason you can't find what you're supposed to do on their list, is because we're not limited to a list. We were all created to go beyond the list and create the life we desire. Isn't that what creativity is, thinking outside the box or even creating it?

Don't box yourself into anyone's expectation of what *they think* you should be. You don't fit in a box because you're bigger than a box. Don't limit God, because He can expand you and take you further than your mind can even imagine.

> *"Now unto him that is able to do exceedingly abundantly above all that we ask or think, according to the power that works in us." Ephesians 3:20*

I could never shake off the vision I had as a little girl, maybe that is why I was unsettled and could never stick to the options that were offered to me.

Talk about feeling awkward and out of place; I just could not fit in. I knew I was going to be a successful businesswoman. What I didn't know was what it looked like. When was it going to happen? And how was I going to get there? I kept asking, seeking, and knocking, trying different doors.

Finally, I obtained an associate degree in business administration and enrolled in a small and private, local university. I knew for sure I would get answers there, since that is where most of the smart and successful people, with careers, get started.

Eventually, I ended up working in the public school system as a substitute teacher, but I knew this was not my purpose, because I felt trapped.

I moved on to become a full-time paraprofessional working with ESE children with autism for a few years and then ESOL (English for speakers of other languages). I did this for 15 years, not because the pay was great, but the School district offered great benefits. I was faithful to do my best at the time, and I loved helping the students, but I knew this was not my calling either. In the back of my mind I was always saying, "There has got to be more to life than this."

Looking back, I see these experiences were teaching me different principles. I learned to wake up early; it taught me discipline because the high school I worked at started at 6:50 am. I learned structure. I learned how to solve problems, and even how to de-escalate situations that could have gone wrong.

I touched the lives of many students at that school, and I Prayed with teachers and staff. So, while I was there, I believe God was working in and through me. The Fruit of the Spirit had to be proven. I had to be faithful where I was, so I would appreciate where He was taking me.

Eventually, I decided to resume my education, and the pursuit for purpose continued. I enrolled at a large university to obtain my bachelor's degree in business administration, and I got lost.

This new university had a huge campus. The classes were so large they met in an auditorium. I was really struggling to keep up and I thought to myself, *perhaps this is not for me.*

I started feeling like college was not the path for me; every time I signed up for a semester, I was just going through the motions. It felt like I was wasting my time. I may have been present in my classes physically, but I was checked out mentally. I can remember sitting in an auditorium filled with students, with the professor lecturing down front, while I thought of other things I could be doing, instead of sitting there.

One of the courses I had taken included a chapter about ADD and ADHD, and as I read about these disorders, I concluded I must have some form of attention deficit. I had always had a hard time paying attention if I had to sit for a long period, I knew I needed to get tested. I was easily distracted, and it was a challenge for me to sit in class and listen to a professor lecture for an entire hour, about something I was not even interested in.

I had pretty much diagnosed myself and knew I needed to see the school psychologist, so I scheduled an appointment. During the first visit, after asking me a few questions, she put me on the computer. I'm assuming this was the diagnostic test to confirm what I thought to be true. Sure enough, she confirmed my suspicions.

She asked me how well I did in school, and I told her I had done okay. I was always a great writer; I think because I had an enormous imagination. I believe that is why I loved English; it was my favorite subject. Although math was not my favorite subject, I did well enough to pass.

She said, "No, I'm wondering how you made it through school without having any special accommodations?" From that day forward, I had a better understanding of how I learn, and why I was struggling.

After failing a couple of semesters, the academic advisor and dean told me, I may want to sit out for a semester or two. I was placed on academic probation; this is a warning that if you don't get your act together, you will be disenrolled from the university.

During my academic probation period, I decided to take advantage of math tutoring for Statistics, Accounting, and Business Math. Needless to say, I did not choose my courses wisely. *Since math was not my strongest point at the time, a humanity or an elective course would have been a better choice.*

I was so overwhelmed, I just shut down mentally. I thought I would be able to handle it if I got additional help; however, I didn't take everything into consideration. All the writing required, meeting homework and project deadlines, responding to discussion boards, then going to my part-time job, and attending bible study. I was completely deprived of any leisure time. This may be the norm for regular college students, but it was not good for me.

Finally, I said to myself "Yasmine, you cannot afford to fail another course, drop the one that is most challenging, you're not going to pass." By the time I had decided to drop the course the add/drop period was over. I was stuck with the class. After trying to get an override from the Dean to drop the course, I had reached my limits and it could not be done. As a result, I ended up failing one of the courses and was dismissed from the university.

I was aimless. The void I was experiencing led to more frustration. I had a burning desire to do something. I had no idea what it was, but I knew it was something greater than what I was doing.

Sometimes, the answer you are looking for is right in your face. I didn't think doing hair was a big deal because it was so common in our community. I was a great braider and made good money as one who specialized in braiding hair, adding extensions, and sewing in weaves or quick bonding hairstyles. Then the thought came to me to go to school for it and so I did!

I loved it! After graduation I found a salon that was looking for licensed beauticians to rent chairs. I met with the owner and negotiated the price I would pay, since I already had clientele from doing hair at home. Working my own hours and scheduling my own appointments, I was an entrepreneur, but didn't even realize it.

Sitting in my chair, clients would share about their lives. I would counsel them and give them my advice, pray for them, and sometimes invite them to know the Lord. I didn't see it at the time, but I was walking in the ministry. Even if they didn't want my prayers, I still prayed as I washed their hair. Even if they didn't know it, the anointing of God flowed through my hands in that shampoo bowl.

After a few years, my fingers and my wrist began hurting and getting stiff. The doctor said it was common amongst beauticians, and if I continued, I would likely end up with arthritis or carpal tunnel. I eventually decided I would not risk long-term issues with my hands and wrists, so as much as I loved doing hair, it was time to move onto something else. It was time for a new season in life.

For some reason, I really believed in my heart that I was going to be a millionaire. Education can add value if you produce something great from it, but it does not tell you what your purpose is; neither does it guarantee you a successful career.

Look at Steve Harvey. He attended college but he never completed it. He became a millionaire, following his dreams to be on TV as a comedian.

Whoopi Goldberg never attended college but landed a role in the movie, *The Color Purple*.

Rachael Ray is a celebrity chef. She stopped attending Pace University after two years to save up money and consider her career goals.

Mark Zuckerberg is one of the founders of Facebook. He dropped out of Harvard University but still became very successful.

Sean Combs, a rapper, record executive, producer, and actor, dropped out of Howard University but became a millionaire.

Don't misunderstand, I am not against education. As a matter of fact, in my opinion, college helps you to become a well-rounded individual because you learn so much about different cultures, religions, and so much more. The challenges I faced were because I did not take the proper time to figure out what I wanted to gain from my education.

My advice, before you attend college, have an idea of what you want to do so you can choose the right track. Otherwise, you will find yourself in an institution with no goal or direction. It's a costly mistake that will be a waste of time.

Anyone can obtain an education from an institution and get a piece of paper. I wanted more than a piece of paper on my wall. I wanted to become a millionaire and give away cars like Oprah Winfrey!

One day, while in prayer, I asked God some specific questions and waited for answers. I was really pressing in because I felt like I *needed* some answers. I was in my mid-twenties, and I had not quite figured out exactly what I was supposed to be doing. I asked God, "What in the world am I supposed to be doing with my life? I need your help. I need some direction. Can you show me what it is?"

After making my request in prayer I sat quietly with the ears of my heart open. Meditation quiets the soul. I said nothing. I uttered not a word. Complete silence. Then I heard these scripture quotes and looked for them in the bible.

> *"For I know the plans and thoughts that I have for you," says the Lord, "plans for peace and well-being and not for disaster, to give you a future and a hope." Jeremiah 29:11*

> *"Or what man is there of you, whom if his son asks for bread, will give him stone? Or if he asks a fish, will he give him a serpent? If you then, being evil, know how to give good gifts unto your children, how much more shall your Father, which is in heaven, give good things to them that ask him?" Matthew 7:9-11*

I asked the Lord for help and direction, and He heard my prayers.

God spoke to my heart and the answer was clear: *Yasmine, I've heard your prayers. I've called you and gifted you to serve my people. I have given you the ability to encourage my people and to let them know I am here, and that I am listening. I've called you to echo my word, to let my people know that I love them. I have called you to bridge the gap. To be a prophet to the nation. I have called you to be the head and to lead. I have called you from amongst them to be separated and set aside for my use and my glory.*

At that moment I felt the power of God so heavy I could not move or speak. It felt like hot honey was pouring over the top of my head and down my entire body. I wept. His presence was so powerful; all I could do was weep and receive what He was saying to me.

That was it, I did not hear anything else. It was not what I wanted to hear, but it was what I needed to hear. I knew in my heart what it was, but I did not want to respond, because then I would have to be accountable. We try to outsmart God, but He knows all and sees all.

Honestly, I was not seeking God for a calling or something to do in ministry for the church, because I felt like I was already serving. I was a Sunday school teacher to little babies and toddlers, and then I became a youth minister for teens. I went on to lead the women's ministry; I led the street witnessing team, assisted with outreach in feeding the homeless, visited and prayed for the sick and shut-in, and served as an assistant to my pastors, assisting in whatever they needed my help with. I was totally available to the Lord. What more could he want from me? I thought I was serving, yet it seemed like He was asking me for more.

What I understood it to mean was; whatever I chose to do with my life, He should be a part of it. Since God is the center of my life, whichever career path I chose, he *would* be part of it. I wanted to tell Him, "I was not talking about that Lord, I'm asking you about my career path. Which direction should I take? I know it's business but what type of business?"

It is important to be very specific in your asking. Effective prayers are precise and targeted, not aimless. When you ask for a specific thing, you release your faith to receive it and you will.

God gives us the ability to make decisions and be creative. He already knows what our capabilities are, He wants us to know what our purpose Is, but He wants us to seek HIM first.

> *"But seek ye first the kingdom of God, and His righteousness; and all these things shall be added unto you."* Matthew 6:33

Seeking means to ask for something from someone. Remember, I was seeking His face for His purpose, and His plans for my life. Not to say I would not have a career or business, but He wanted to emphasize what He called me to do, and it was all wrapped in the words He spoke to me that day. It was up to me to align myself with His word, purpose, and plans for my life.

It was a breath of fresh air to hear that He had a plan for my future, one filled with hope. It was a sense of relief. I no longer had to walk as though I had no direction. The plan for my entire future was in Him, and He placed it in me before I was born. Now my prayers are more specific. I seek God to lead and show me His plans for my future, so I can align my life with his plans, and so that I can prosper.

The vision I had when I was a little girl came to me again, but this time it was clearer. What I saw in that vision was now confirmed with His word. Whichever career path or business I chose, He was going to be the center of it all. I would be successful if I follow His Kingdom principles.

> *"But thou shalt remember the Lord thy God: for it is He that gives you power to make wealth, that He may confirm his covenant which He swore to your fathers as it is this day." Deuteronomy 8:18*

I am currently living out the vision I had of myself of being a successful businesswoman, as an entrepreneur. It is not without God being the center of it at all. I acknowledge Him in every aspect of my life and in everything I do, because He is the one who directs my path. He knows everything!

Our personal experience in finding and purchasing a home was very challenging, and it led me down a new path. Now I find myself encouraging and praying with people in the process of serving them, in a new way. As a real estate agent, it allows me to follow my passion in serving families while solving their problems and meeting their real estate needs. I pray for my clients, the realtors I meet, and every transaction. I am the praying realtor, the one who encourages and walks people through the entire process. It's all ministry when serving people, in any industry or career path that requires some level of service.

So many other things have been birthed since I began asking, seeking, and knocking. I've received so much more than what I could have ever imagined. I have found more than what I was looking for and so many doors have opened for me. I believe everything I went through was to lead me to this point. Everything served a purpose.

During the process I discovered that I am, among other things, an entrepreneur, an exhorter, an encourager, a public speaker, a philanthropist, an author, and an ambassador of the Kingdom of God — and still discovering so much more.

To find your purpose in life, ask your creator! He already has the perfect plan for your life. All you must do is ask and receive it. Seek and you will find it. Knock and the door will open.

EMBRACING ME

Awakening Your Gift

REFLECTION JOURNALING

Take a notebook and begin writing down what comes to your mind when you ask yourself the following question(s). Be completely honest with yourself.

- Do you know what your specific purpose is? Write down what you envision yourself doing.
- How are you pursuing it? Are you passive or passionately aggressive about obtaining it?
- How much time are you willing to invest in yourself?

- What special talent can you use to get you closer if you work at it consistently?

- How much money are you willing to invest in yourself?

EMBRACING ME

CHAPTER 4
Believing in Prayer

As you pray to the Lord things will start happening in your life. Do not become discouraged if the door does not open for you immediately. Some open doors will be shut and it's okay. You may have to make some adjustments to get the results you are believing God for.

I believe prayer aligns you with the will of God, so you can walk through open doors.

> *"And the key of the House of David will I lay upon his shoulder; so he shall open, and none shall shut; and he shall shut, and none shall open." Isaiah 22:22*

Whatever door God opens for you, is for you. No one can shut the door God has opened and none can open what God has shut. Everything is by design and is for an appointed time. Work on what you can work on while you're waiting. Do something. Faith without works is dead. You must apply your faith to your works, so it can manifest the will of God.

Prayers can be answered in many different ways. As a matter of fact, most of the time God does not answer our prayers in the way or fashion we think He should. It's good to be open-minded and flexible.

When I was contemplating a career change out of cosmetology, I knew I was at a fork in the road and it was time for change, so I prayed for guidance. I asked, "Lord, I know there is more to life than this because my heart is telling me there is more. What is it? What should I be doing right now?"

At this point, I had experienced life as an entrepreneur and loved it. I knew a business career was what I wanted for myself, and I remembered my husband mentioning real estate school. I wondered if this was the direction God was calling me, so again I prayed. *"God, I yield to your plans, purpose, and perfect will for my life. I believe all things are working together for my good. Everything I do, prospers."*

My shift took place when I finally accepted whatever His will was for my life. I was tired of trying to figure it out and doing things the way I thought best. Following his will is easier and a lot less exhausting.

When you pray and ask God to lead you, He will. You must be willing to follow the dream when He does lead you. It's not always going to be what you thought, but God will show you enough to fire you up so you can move forward.

Something happened after we finally purchased our new construction home, built from scratch. That is when I heard the voice of the Lord tell me to help His people purchase their homes.

God planted the vision in my heart to become a Realtor, so I took the course and passed the state exam. I hung my license in September of 2019 and landed my first deal, representing my buyer, and closed in November 2019. It simply prayed and then took the steps necessary to move forward. Business seemed to flow naturally for me.

Since we had struggled trying to purchase our first home, I loved being the resolution to people's real estate problems and was passionate about helping the 1st time home buyer get their property.

I am not just a realtor. I am a real estate agent on an assignment. I am here to solve people's real estate problems. I provide more than a service. I bring value. I serve them.

When you start living and walking your dream, because you believe, it is noticeable. All you must do is follow the dream you believe in. *The question is what do you dream of becoming?*

Even though I was living my purpose, I felt that we

would be relocating. I said to the Holy Spirit, *"If this is you, then you will open doors for us."* I felt it heavily in my heart that we were not going to be where we were for long. I did not understand it, but I knew it was the Holy Spirit because there was a sense of peace. The peace of God surpasses all understanding.

You may not understand what God is doing in your life, but just trust Him. You won't be made ashamed.

> *"Whoever believes in Him {whoever adheres to, trusts in, and relies on Him} will not be disappointed {in his expectations}." Romans 10:11*

No one took me seriously when I said I was moving. I knew it was Him. I asked God to confirm it in His word showing me it was truly of Him and not of myself. I opened my word exactly on this scripture.

> *"Go away from your country and from your relatives and from your father's house to the land which I will show you; And I will make you a great nation, and I will bless you abundantly and make your names great (exalted and distinguished); And you shall be blessing, a source of great good to others." Genesis 12:1&2*

For an entire year I had been telling different people, my family, church family, and friends, we would be moving soon. They would ask where and my response was always, "I don't know, but we will be moving soon."

Doors started opening as we yielded to the Holy Spirit's voice. God does everything in order. At the time, my husband and I had been youth ministers for over eight years. The Lord had us grooming two other leaders who would be taking over, so they could make the necessary adjustments as we transitioned.

We held other positions as well, but people were slowly filling those positions. I led the praise and worship team for years and, suddenly, He sent us more worshippers that could lead. He gradually transitioned us from most of the positions we were holding. We could see the hand of God moving things around.

Although I had been saying we were moving, my husband was not quite on board yet. He didn't want to move because he had been working for the criminal courts for several years and was making a decent living. The money was decent but the cost of living in Miami was ridiculous, and higher than both of our incomes combined could afford, but God had a plan.

I went into prayer and asked the Lord if He would deal with His son Fabian, because he was not having it. A few days later my husband said, "We are moving."

I took a double take and said, "Okay, what happened?" Of course, I knew what had happened, but I wanted him to confirm it. Holy Spirit dealt with him and told him, "It's not about location, but it's about my word going forth." In that moment, he knew exactly what God was saying to him: *We were relocating*!

Talk about God speaking expressively. I smiled and winked at heaven, as if to say, "God you are awesome!"

It happened quickly. Doors were opening left and right. I mean, as soon as we were both on the same page, a door opened, and we completed an application to lease a house in Lee County.

Ever since we relocated from Broward County to Lee County, it has been blessings after blessings. We went from faith to faith and glory to glory. After putting the money down to lease the property, we only had about $1,000.00 to our names. For three months straight, God provided for us, and we lacked nothing. As a matter of fact, it seemed like we had more with less.

We were blown away to see how God took care of us supernaturally. It pays to obey God. Doors opened for the both of us simultaneously. First my husband got a job, then I got one. Everything just fell in place, and we lacked for nothing. He sent random people to give us rental money, utility money, and people brought food and groceries. Everything we needed, we asked for, we believed, and He provided it.

I remember asking God specifically about a particular event I was planning. I asked him, "God if this is your will for me to do this now, confirm it." A day or two later, someone called me to say God had laid on their heart to give us a specific amount. I looked up and smiled because that was the exact amount, I had put down to book the event. God told her to tell me He had heard my prayers. He was with me and would provide for the vision He had given to me. I knew this was His confirmation!

What you pray for and ask for in secret, God will manifest the answer through whomever, whenever, and however He wills. I had not spoken to anyone but God. I knew it was the Holy Spirit confirming Himself to me. His word was established by two or three witnesses, so it was settled. I had a peace in my heart that God was with me, for me, and everything was working out for my good.

Someone once told me they don't ask God for anything because He deals with enough. I gave her this perplexed look as if to say, *What*? *He is GOD! Well, that's why you are where you are, because you have not asked of Him. You're trying to do things with your own strength.* Clearly, she was in error and not rightly divining the word of truth. He tells us to ASK!

Often, people have the wrong concept of who our God is. Mixing your personal feelings, ideology, and theory with what has already been defined and established, can leave you in a confused state. When you ask God, He will confirm and answer with his word. If the word aligns with his scriptures and there is a peace in your heart, you're good. God won't leave you guessing.

The word of God, (the Bible) is our owner's manual giving us specific instructions, answers, and direction. It teaches, corrects, and is perfect for all things. Everything we need is in the owner's manual of our life, the Holy Bible. Read it, for in it is your life.

We've heard the saying so many times, the acronym for BIBLE: Basic Instruction Before Leaving Earth. Yet it doesn't really sink in until we align our heart, mind, and spirit with His word. How could something so simple be so complicated?

He gave me other scriptures validating me, and the more I read, the more confident I became about myself.

"Yasmine," he told me, *"I will teach you everything you need to know. Seek my face, read my words, and follow my instructions."* In seeking God, He will encourage you with His word.

Yes, you will need to hold fast to some of those encouraging words because the distance between asking and receiving can be a few days, months, or years. In fact, holding fast to the promises of God will remind you that God has not forgotten.

From my experience, it's better to write down what the Lord tells you, so you can always refer to what He said. This helped me a lot. No matter how shaky and iffy things got, I stood on His word. This is why I learned to speak His word; it is powerful.

Words are powerful, always choose your words wisely. Be careful what comes out of your mouth because it will manifest. Whether it be good or bad.

In the worst situation I encountered (a near death

experience), I spoke the word of God over myself. I was having really bad heart palpitations; as a result, I would have severe panic attacks. My husband would have to call the paramedics, or I would end up at the ER.

During one ER visit, after many of these episodes, a doctor came in and asked me if I had ever been tested for Graves' disease. I was like, *what*? He said they didn't have the means to do the testing there, but recommended I visit the hospital across town after my discharge. I did just that and was admitted to the cardiac unit, bed ridden with a heart monitor and catheter for five days.

Those five days were challenging. I can recall sitting in a quiet place, just meditating, not saying a word. And I hear God say, *"You were fearfully and wonderfully made. You are chosen. You are a royal warrior from a lineage of the royal priesthood. You were created in my image and likeness. Specially designed with unique characteristics, features, and traits. You are unique even down to your DNA: cells, molecules, and blood type. Not even your sister or brother are exactly alike. YOU are different and that's perfectly fine. I created you that way."*

Who are you to tell your creator you don't like His masterpiece?

> *"For you formed my inward parts; you knitted me together in my mother's womb. I praise you, for I am fearfully and wonderfully made." Psalms 139: 13-14*

"You are more than enough. You are sufficient, Yasmine." There, I got it. The light bulb came on. As I began seeking the face of God, He spoke to me through His word.

> *"But seek first the kingdom of God and His righteousness, and all these things will be added to me." Matthew 6:33*

That was it. All I had to do was seek Him because everything I needed was in Him. I align myself with the creator by simply getting into His word.

Read the owner's manual, the Bible? You mean to tell me all the answers and questions I had were in this manual (BIBLE) the whole time? Yes!

Just as Chevy is the manufacturer of our Tahoe Truck, God is the manufacturer of His people. In order to get the best use out of the vehicle, it is best to read the owner's manual before adding the wrong gas or oil. Likewise, one should seek their creator for the blueprint of his or her life. The more I read, the more I discovered about myself and who I was, and what my purpose is.

There was nothing wrong with going to college. It is a great tool. I was hoping college would tell me who I was and what my purpose was. No, college was a tool or a resource where I could obtain information, skills, and research to add to my foundation, of what God had already created me with from the beginning.

The moment I began seeking God's face and reading my owner's manual (HOLY BIBLE) I had more clarity and direction. This was my foundation to build my knowledge in Him. This is where I discovered who I really was. Pressing on in prayer. Seeking his face. Meditating on His word gave me such an undeniable peace. He is embedded in my heart, mind, body, and soul, God's word is the sure foundation. He added more value to my true self.

In addition, I continued personal development, disciplining myself to be the best version of me. I became a student who was always learning and applying. I continued seeking wise counsels, attending seminars to learn from other people's experiences. In all reality, I found that some things were just being confirmed repeatedly. Some people are just more skillful or knowledgeable in a particular field than others because they have years of experience and have invested their time to learn.

Neither man nor an institution can tell you who you are or what your purpose is. They can only affirm or confirm. They can add more value to what God has already placed within you. They can even stir the gift inside of you by enlightening you through words of knowledge, wisdom, and experience, or challenge you to tap into your true source.

Ultimately, it's up to you how successful you become or how far you go in life. We were created with the ability to obtain everything we need to be successful and productive. Unless we tap into the source that will reveal God's plan and purpose for our lives, then we are just existing and not living.

In this next stage of my life, I am passionate about people being their best selves. God has called me to serve and encourage his people, exhort them, and let them know God has a plan and a purpose for their lives. It is my hope that, after reading this book, you will be compelled to go after your purpose as a deer pants for streams of water. That you will have a hunger no one else can fill or a thirst only God can quench.

Your hunger must be greater than your appetite. Seek God's face as if your life is dependent upon it because it is!

Set your eyes on God. Don't worry about what everyone else is doing. When God downloads his plans for your life in your heart, you won't have to worry about what others are doing, saying, or thinking. God's purpose is burning in your heart, and it has precedent over everything else!

Your assignment will be enough for you, trust me! His purpose becomes priority over everything you could possibly imagine. You'll be focused on what his will, plans, and purpose for your life are and where they will lead and guide you. You won't feel a release until you fulfill your purpose.

It's like a woman who is giving birth to a child. You can feel when the contraction is coming so you bear down and position yourself to push. You do not feel comfortable until that child comes forth.

So, the question I was asking in the beginning, was not my concern. God has THE HOW it's going to get done. When you obey His voice, follow His instructions, and wait on Him, it will get done. Ultimately that is more pleasing to God than anything.

Hear me; you will never look at life the same way

again. Your perspective on life will be so clear. You will not get easily distracted because you know you're on an assignment and you must please Him.

Look up to the hills because that is where your help is coming from — from God, not man. He may use man to answer your prayers, but you should always seek God first concerning your life.

He will answer you through his word, the Holy Bible. He said, by two or three witnesses, let every word be established.

God will confirm through His word and people. That is exactly what He did when we sought His face. He led us here and He provided for us.

Everything you need is in the owner's manual. All we must do is read it, follow his instructions, and believe in the power of prayer.

EMBRACING ME

Awakening Your Gift

REFLECTION JOURNALING

Take a notebook and begin writing down what comes to your mind when you ask yourself the following question(s). Be completely honest with yourself.

- What do you believe? Your faith is not for what's possible, it's the substance of things hoped for, and the evidence of things not seen.
- Write down a clear vision of what you are hoping for. Say it aloud, recite it, visualize yourself doing it.

EMBRACING ME

Awakening Your Gift

STEP 3: RESETTING YOU

EMBRACING ME

CHAPTER 5
Transforming Your Mind

Factory Reset

I used to be a fighter and still am to an extent, I have just changed how I fight and who I fight for now. I used to fight because it felt good. It was my way of releasing anger, stress, and frustration. In addition to being raised in a challenging, hostile environment, I had also picked up some bad habits.

As much as I hated what I saw, I replicated it. I mimicked the same poor behavior I saw at home, so I became verbally and physically abusive toward others. It was a learned behavior.

I had many fights. I don't remember most of them because I would black out completely. When the spirit of rage took over, I no longer had control.

One day, a young man in my high school science class called me the "B" word. Immediately, without even a thought, in a rage I picked up the desk and launched it at him, to teach him a lesson. I ran out of the classroom as fast as I could. He chased me down the hall until I was eventually stopped by an administrator and a school security guard, to explain what happened. We both got in trouble.

About two years later, I accepted the Lord Jesus Christ as my personal Lord and Savior. In my heart I knew something had taken place. It felt like something had lifted off me and I felt lighter. I was changed, instantly my life became different.

As I matured, I recognized my problem, and I asked the Holy Spirit to please help me. To teach me how to overcome and replace this bad habit with good habits. However, during my last year of high school, something finally changed.

When I surrendered my life to God, the old me was gone. I was a new person. I had a hunger for His word, like a person who was starving for food. My mind was being renewed as I read His word every single day. I just could not get enough. I pondered on it, I couldn't stop talking about it, and walked in it.

In the Bible the book of Romans talks about not being conformed to this world. *We are to be transformed by the renewing of our mind.* It is by testing we are able to discern the will of God; those things which are good and acceptable and perfect.

I submerged myself in Him because I loved the experience and the encounter. It was undeniably transformational. I was in love with Jesus!

It was as if someone hit the factory reset button.

I got to start all over again. I felt like a brand-new person. I was no longer a walking, ticking bomb, full of anger and rage. I was full of so much love, I wanted to share it with everyone.

The more time I spent in His presence, reading His word daily, the more my mind was being renewed. Although I had taken the first step, renewing my mind daily was still a process.

The way I used to think changed. I no longer felt like I was on an assignment to shred someone to pieces. I had calmed down drastically. That does not mean I did not have moments, but those moments started to become a thing of the past.

I honestly had no desire to be the way I used to be. I wanted to please God. I wanted to be more like Him. I was even asking myself who was this new person in my body. As I mentioned, one time I felt like I was losing my mind.

There would be situations that took me to a dark place, one where I wanted to revert to the old person. I resisted and I cried instead. I cried because I did not know how to respond during a disagreement or altercation. I was tempted to go there, but I couldn't do it. Resist the devil and he will flee.

I went to God several times sobbing, asking Him what was wrong with me. I encountered people I should have cursed out or given a piece of my mind, but I just couldn't. What was I supposed to do, let people walk all over me? Why were these people trying me? I did not know it at the time, but I was being tried by fire. Every good work must be tried.

The Holy Spirit was teaching me there was a better way to communicate. I felt like He was allowing people to take advantage of me, and I was embarrassed because I did not know how to effectively communicate.

It was pride. In the back of my mind, I said to myself, "Wait a minute, this person apparently does not know who I am. They really don't know what I am capable of doing to them."

Then I heard the Holy Spirit respond to my thoughts, *No Yasmine they don't know who you are. Tell me, who are you?*

I was shocked that He responded to my thoughts. I knew where He was going with the question because it came with an answer. *You are my child; you represent the Kingdom of Heaven.*

I thought to myself, *I definitely do not want to misrepresent you because I love you.*

He said, *exactly. When you love me more than the sin (your weakness), you will not give in to your fleshly desires, but instead, you will be led by the Holy Spirit. When you received the Holy Spirit, you received power! Walk in the Spirit and you will not fulfill the lust of your flesh. Bring your body under subjection. You have the power to do so.*

I remember reading, fasting and praying weakens the flesh and strengthens the spirit. So, I fasted and prayed all the time. I wanted to walk in the Spirit.

One of the ways I changed was by changing my environment. I moved away from what I knew was my weakness. The Lord made a way for me. My pastors did not have any children, so they took me in. But I believe the Lord had instructed them to do so. Living in their house was a different world. Something I had to get used to.

Granted, there were countless times where I felt like I was not a believer. Sometimes, I did not feel worthy of His grace, mercy, and love. But those were just thoughts. I learned how to defeat those negative thoughts by speaking the word of God over my life. *There is no condemnation to them who are in Christ Jesus.* God loves me and He forgave me. He does not remember my past. Old things have passed away and I am new.

The closer I got to Jesus the stronger I became. Other things I slowly separated from where my family and friends. There comes a season in your life when, if you want to see a change, you must be willing to make small adjustments. Small adjustments yield massive results.

I started hanging out less because I had no desire to party and meet at the club anymore. Those things did not interest me. I loved my family, but they knew my trigger points, and I knew I was not strong enough to resist some of the temptations that would put me in the wrong place spiritually. It was not easy, but I knew if I wanted to change, I would have to change what I was doing and who I was surrounding myself with.

I came to realize it was not in a feeling; it is in believing in His word that says we were redeemed when Christ died on the cross once and for all. As a baby Christian, I did not fully grasp that concept. But the more I pressed into reading His word, fellowshipping with Him, and spending time with Him, I began to develop into an entirely new person inside and out. What was inside was spilling outward. He cleanses us from the inside out.

Here is the ironic part. After being transformed, I had a very hard time adjusting. God had changed my heart and I wrestled against it sometimes. I felt like I had lost the old, tough exterior person; I did not know how to engage in a disagreement without crying.

I recall getting into altercations or disagreements with people, and I would begin sobbing. I was like, *Wait. Why am I crying?* I used to curse or hit them so that I gained control of the situation. At least that was what I thought then, in truth I had no control.

Upset about the new development, I went into prayer and asked God, *"Why are you embarrassing me? This is not cool. I feel like you're making me soft. Why am I responding this way? I don't want people taking advantage of me. I would love to give them a piece of my mind and get them off me."* It was a confusing time.

The Holy Spirit nudged me and said in a soft manner, very gently, *"Yasmine, you are a new person. Do not reach back for what's familiar. The old nature will try to rise up and resist your new nature, but all you have to do is yield to me. Focus on me. Take a deep breath and think about something good and pleasant."*

> *"And put on the new self (regenerated and renewed nature), created in God's image, godlike in the righteousness and holiness of the truth (living to express to God your gratitude for your salvation)."* Ephesians 4:24

He had to literally coach me through the break down process and calm me down. You could compare my personality to *The Incredible Hulk™* when I was mad and Bruce Banner when I was calm. I realized my old nature, I did not have the power to control my actions; however, with my new nature, I had POWER which gave me control. I just had to be willing to resist the temptation of what I was used to doing in times past. I could not believe who this new person was. Resist the enemy and he will flee. Whatever scripture that gave me strength and courage, I clung to it and made it mine.

I can recall seeing myself respond to certain situations where I know the old Yas would have risen and given it to them. But that wouldn't glorify God. Plus, the conviction of knowing that I would be misrepresented Him.

Resetting your mind is simply regenerating and renewing it daily by reading the word. This does not mean that I was perfect, but I was striving for it by pressing towards the mark of the prize of the high calling which is in Christ Jesus.

Renewing my mind showed me I was growing gracefully in Him. What used to strike a nerve and have me jumping in someone's face or beating them to a pulp, didn't anymore.

I had been a believer for about ten years, and I remember having an altercation with my younger sister. My husband and I had just moved into a townhouse and lived there for about three months, when we received foreclosure papers on the house. We called the landlord to ask what was going on, and he confessed he knew it was coming, and told us we would have to move out.

We had just paid a lump sum (first, last, and security) and we did not have that kind of money saved up to do it again. We were both working, and we made enough to pay our bills and buy groceries, but not enough to build savings.

We put our things in storage and my mom gave up

her room in the family home for us to stay, so we could save enough to get another place. I was uncomfortably pregnant with my second child and living out of one bedroom with my husband and our one-year-old daughter. But we made it work.

One day my sister stopped by for a visit and made some comments I didn't like, about things that did not concern her, and I snapped. I forgot I was pregnant and launched at her with a blow to her face. The next thing you know, we were fighting.

My other siblings, who were still living at home, were screaming, "Yasmine, no, stop, stop, you are pregnant!"

I let her have it. Finally, they pulled me off her and I was screaming at the top of my lungs, "I'm leaving! I am not staying here. Nobody deserves to be treated like this."

I called my husband's job, screaming at his supervisor on the phone. "Tell Fabian to come and get me, come, and get me now! I want to leave NOW." I was livid. My ears were burning, my heart was palpitating, and I was upset! My siblings tried to calm me down, but it was not happening.

When Fabian arrived, I finally calmed down and felt

a sense of peace. I cried because I was so embarrassed that I had allowed my little sister to get the best of me. I could not justify myself at all. I was ashamed. I had totally forgotten I was pregnant and endangering myself and my son. How stupid was that?

After I had calmed down and thought about what I had done, I not only prayed and asked for forgiveness, but I also called my sister and apologized.

This was a learning experience for me, of course. I learned to never allow anyone to affect my character. Everything is a choice. I can choose to remove myself from a situation, or I can allow my flesh to override the Holy Spirit. Whichever one you yield to; you give power to. I was not interested in yielding my members to the enemy.

I realized it is imperative to constantly reset your mind. Okay, my response was not the best, so let me make some adjustments.

Reflection is always a good opportunity to reset, restart, and do it better than before. There is no condemnation to those who are in Christ Jesus, conviction comes to give you an opportunity to correct, not to punish you.

I'd rather look like a complete fool and humble myself instead of being prideful and bring shame to the kingdom of God. If I am representing Him, I don't need to defend myself. He will defend and protect me because he is my rock, fortress, and protector.

According to Ephesians 6:11-18, I am fully armored with the whole armor of God. If I stay in the high place and abide in Him, the enemy can't get to me. The enemy must make me come down to his level. Through the power of transformation, and the daily renewal of my mind, I made a conscious decision not to stoop to the enemy's level.

That does not mean I am perfect. It simply means I am trusting Him to help me every single day, because I can do all things through Christ who strengthens me. *If I make a mistake or fall short, I'll repent and ask God forgiveness, and keep moving.*

I am indeed a changed person, and I will not let my flesh rob me of the very same thing I have already conquered and overcame by the blood of Jesus.

> *"The weapons of our ware are not carnal, but they are mighty in God for pulling down strongholds, casting down imaginations, and*

every high thing that exalteth itself against the knowledge of God and bringing into captivity every thought to the obedience of Christ." 2 Corinthians 10:4-5

Stacking Good Habits

It's in our nature to develop habits, some of them are good, and some are not. In the book *Developing the Leader in You,* by John Maxwell, he mentions that leaders should learn to stack good habits. One of the habits is growth.

"Choosing to grow is important, but that decision is not enough to create change on its own. We need to acknowledge that growth is a gradual process and make that process part of our daily practice. That means we need to establish the habit of growing on a consistent basis." – John Maxwell

For me, this starts with becoming aware of the habits that serve my purposes and those that do not. It's not easy getting rid of habits that do not serve me, so I follow a simple system to help me.

I came across the book *Miracle Morning* by Hal Elrod. He talks about the 6 S.A.V.E.R.S™: Silence, Affirmations, Visualization, Exercise, Reading, and Scribing. Since I had already developed some good habits, like waking up an hour earlier every morning to center myself with prayer, reading, and journaling, I thought why not stack a few more good habits, to replace some old ones.

I will be honest with you. Some habits are easier to break than others. Ultimately, I believe it takes determination and making up your mind to do it.

I used to wake up at 6 AM. Then I realized, I was not giving myself enough time before starting my day. I decided to make a small but challenging adjustment and wake up at 5 AM. I intentionally set my alarm for 4:45 AM, so I could hit my snooze button at least twice. I eventually adapted to waking up an hour earlier than my normal time. This gave me time to incorporate 3 more things I wanted to add: Affirmations, Visualization and Exercising.

I added another good habit as well. After declaring my affirmations, I wrote 5 things that I am thankful for. I got this one from one of Oprah Winfrey's Motivation Videos.

In total I have 7 things I do every single morning. They are a part of my mind being transformed, and it resets me for a brand-new day. Then I am clear and ready for the 5 tasks in my calendar each day.

Of course, it doesn't mean that I will hit every goal of the day, but I use this method to help me stay focused and on track, since I can easily be distracted, busy, and not productive.

When you know who you are and whose you are, you carry yourself accordingly. I know that I am an Ambassador of the Kingdom of God, and I will carry myself as such.

EMBRACING ME

Awakening Your Gift

REFLECTION JOURNALING

Take a notebook and begin writing down what comes to mind when you ask yourself the following question(s). Be completely honest with yourself.

- What does transforming your mind mean?
- What can you do to help yourself during this process?
- Can you continue living the same way and expect different results?

Some things happen suddenly, and others may progress in time.

- Are you willing to put in the work every day by making small adjustments to obtain massive results?

EMBRACING ME

Awakening Your Gift

STEP 4: THE LIBERTY

EMBRACING ME

CHAPTER 6
Walking in Power

There is nothing like walking in liberty. Being free from the oppressive restrictions imposed on our society by authority. I have the right to be free from anything that imposes restrictions on me. Liberty gives you the power to be true to yourself.

When I hear the word *power* I think of authority and someone who is influential. Some people are abusive of their power and use it maliciously while others use it to influence and impact the lives of other people.

The twelve disciples were given power and authority over all demons and to cure diseases (Luke 9:1), and they used it to impact the lives of others.

A police officer receives power and authority from the department in which he serves. They go through an academy for special training and during the graduation ceremony they are given the power and authority to serve, protect, and enforce the law. Along with that, they are given a certain attire, a uniform which visually represents their power and authority, and usually, a marked vehicle which also represents a form of authority.

Whenever we see a cop in the same lane or driving

behind us, we tend to slow down and drive the speed limit or below it. Why do we slow down? Because we know they have a level of authority to pull us over if we break the law by driving over the speed limit. Without power and authority, a police officer would not be as effective.

Having the Holy Spirit is similar, but greater. After receiving the Holy Spirit, I had received *power* and *authority*! No, people may not slowdown in their vehicles when they see me, but they know something is different about me.

Most people can sense power and authority when someone carries it inside of them and they show reverence. This was my experience. After I had an encounter with receiving the Holy Spirit, I carried power and authority.

I remember visiting someone at their home who had missed a few church services. I had already known she was going through something, but when I sat down on the couch in the living room, we just began talking. I remember encouraging her and building up her faith with the word of God.

The moment we began to pray, an unclean spirit began to manifest. She went from sitting on the couch to slithering on the floor like a snake. As a new believer in Christ, I was not expecting that at all. The flesh, the human side of me, was shocked and afraid for a moment. Then almost immediately something rose up in me and rebuked that unclean spirit and commanded it to come out of her in the name of Jesus.

Honestly, I had no idea what I was doing because this was unexpected, and I had no personal training for this type of situation. No, the Holy Spirit was quickened in me because I had power and authority. Within seconds that foul unclean spirit came out of her and she was free!

After that event, I was on an assignment to serve and nurture her. She was actually my very first disciple without me even knowing. I watched her grow and saw the Lord do great things in her life. After fifteen years, she is still on fire for Jesus. She loves Him and walks in her ministry.

I pattern my life after Jesus because I love Him. This is what He commissioned us to do. Go out and preach the gospel and compel men unto Him. He said we would do greater works in his name, and I believe it.

We love to look up to others and admire them as powerful and influential people. One of those people whom I admired the most growing up was my mom. To me, she is the perfect example of a virtuous woman. I admire her strength.

With a middle school education, she entered the United States with a plan to prosper. She worked minimum wage jobs, and raised ten children, three born in Haiti and seven in the US. She owned real estate and managed her money like an investor. She taught her eight girls and two sons to never wait for anyone to give them anything. Whatever you want in life, work for it; she always said, "Get up and go get it." She would say, "I don't trust in man, I trust in God. I could not raise you all, pay a mortgage and deal with life without Jesus. I made God my best friend."

I love my mother and, yes, she is to be admired, but I am not my mother. What she did was her path. Her life and her story, not mine. Certainly, there are absolutely, without a shadow of doubt, positive traits I inherited from my mother, but I am not her. My mom is also an introvert. She begged me to be like her in that manner, but I couldn't.

I love interacting with people. I am adventurous and

love to see what's on the other side. God created me with unique characteristics that make me who I am. I am different. My energy is high, and I love helping people.

He has made me an influential woman, even though I never thought of myself as such. There are so many lives that have been changed because of the power that lies inside of me. I take NO credit. I am just a vessel. Humbled that He would use me in such a powerful way.

As leaders, God has given us the ability to do something in a particular way and the capacity to direct or influence the behavior of others or the course of an event. God wants us to act in the authority He has bestowed upon us. I read about His power, and had experienced His power, but had never really exercised it.

> *"For God gave us a spirit not of fear but of power and love and self-control."* 2 Timothy 1:7

I want to focus on the word *power*. It is the ability to do something or act in a particular way. According to Websters dictionary, power is also defined as the capacity or ability to direct or influence the behavior of others or the course of an event.

The more I yielded to the Holy Spirit, the more I began seeing a change in my life. As a result, some people I came in contact with also changed. Lives I was influencing yet did not recognize at the time.

That's what power does. When you turn the lights on with the flick of a switch, you don't see the current running through the conductor to transmit the electricity into light. It is the same way with having the power of God inside of us.

Jesus said, "After the Holy Spirit has come upon you, you will have *power.*" Power is accessible to everyone, but it's which power you choose to yield to that makes a difference. My encounter with being filled with the Holy Spirit not only changed my life, but it also changed the lives of the people I encountered.

I remember a particular young lady in our church. We had similar backgrounds, having Haitian parents, trying to raise their children in the US with Haitian culture and values. She was going through a rough time with her mom, and I understood it all too well.

I shared with her my experience of being rebellious, defiant, and full of anger and rage. I took her under my wing, and she became like a little sister to me. At the time I didn't even know that I was mentoring her, but I was.

One day, she called me crying and asked if I could help her. She had gotten into an altercation with her mom, and she was going to jail. She asked if I could please come and get her child. I thought to myself, *why would she call me of all people? What about her family or other relatives?* I am not next of kin or related to her. I had not known her that long for her to even consider me as being a temporary guardian of her child. Yet I felt compelled by the Holy Spirit to help wherever I could. My husband and I went to court and agreed to have temporary custody of her son until she was released.

This is when I discovered that the power of influence was effectively working in my life. I had the ability to act in the authority of representing this young lady in court as a positive, influential person in her life.

A few weeks later we returned to the court requesting permission for the young lady to live with us, so she could interact with her child. Although all her rights had not been restored, we wanted her to be present with her child.

This was going to be a huge challenge; I knew the power of influence had the ability to change her, if she was willing. If she could see how my husband and I lived and raised our children, she would glean from us and hopefully pick up some good habits.

It took time but what appeared to be a challenge, taking in a toddler with a troubled teen mother, turned out to be one of the most rewarding experiences I have ever had.

She went back to school and obtained her GED and completed a degree in the medical field. She got her own place and became very successful. She has an amazing bond with her son who is now a teen. She called me and my husband a few years ago to say thank you.

She said, "Thank you for taking me and my son into your home. Thank you for never giving up on me and giving me a chance. At the time I did not understand why you were so hard on me, but now I understand it was because you really loved me and wanted the best for me and my son. I appreciate you and will never forget what you did for me and my child. You taught me how to carry myself as a young lady, how to cook, clean, parent my child, and most of all, have a relationship with God. You were my example and I truly thank God for you."

I replied, "All glory goes to God. We are just vessels he wants to demonstrate his power through, to impact the lives of others."

I share this experience because the power to influence someone else's behavior is best done through leading by example. I believe she was transformed by what she saw us doing.

There's an old saying, "Do as I say and not as I do." Wrong, wrong, wrong! People learn from what they see you doing. Talk is cheap. You will know a person by the fruit they bare and produce. She witnessed our lifestyle as believers. We really practiced it and lived it wholeheartedly.

A lot of people can preach and talk about the word of God, but many are not willing to live a disciplined lifestyle that mirrors the word of God.

Seeing someone transform their life because of my influence taught me how to appreciate and value the gift that was given to me. Leading by example is the greatest power one can use to influence others. It is powerful.

EMBRACING ME

Awakening Your Gift

REFLECTION JOURNALING

Take a notebook and begin writing down what comes to your mind when you ask yourself the following question(s). Be completely honest with yourself.

- Which power is being exemplified in your life?
- What type of influence do you have in the lives of others? Is it good or bad?
- Is the POWER OF GOD being demonstrated in your life?

Remember you are responsible for what God has entrusted to you.

EMBRACING ME

CHAPTER 7
Walking in Love

What's love got to do with it, right? Love has everything to do with everything. Love is the reason why I am here. It was God's love that transformed my life completely. Love is powerful.

> "God so loved the world that He gave His only begotten son, that whosoever believes in him shall not perish but have everlasting life." John 3:16

Although love was given freely to us, it was the hardest thing for me to receive and comprehend. Since I could not receive this gracious, unconditional love, it was pretty darn hard for me to give what I really did not possess. Our human nature does not understand how we can love without it being reciprocated.

You know how it is; if you do this for me, I'll do that for you. There was always a selfish motive. What's in it for me? Seriously, *what am I getting in return*, was the way I thought!

Who wants to be that vulnerable and put themselves out there, with no protection at all? My walls were made of steel so nothing could hurt me. Life experience taught me how to build barriers around my heart. As a result, nothing could come in and I had nothing to give.

This is why we must be born again. Our minds must be renewed, and our hearts transformed. This is the only way we can receive and accept His love. Under my old nature without Christ, my love was conditional. If you showed me love, I'd show you love.

That is not the true definition of love. *Love is an intense feeling of deep affection; a great interest and pleasure in something or someone.*

Why would I open my heart and give someone else that much power? After being taken advantage of and abused, I made sure that I would never, ever, be that stupid again. Heartbroken from my first *boo thang*. Head over heels, yes, I was madly in love, and I thought he was in love with me too, until I found out that I was *his main chick*, not the *only chick* on his side.

I was crushed, humiliated, and embarrassed. To think I was his one and only and I wasn't. I was furious with myself for being so naive and gullible. Before you know it, unforgiveness quietly settled in and I shut down. Shutting down was easy for me because I had surrendered my life to the Lord.

At the time I was not entertaining anyone. I was saved, single, and serving. Pride kicked in because I felt like I had it all together. Although I was attracting nice men, I would turn them away self-righteously. "I'm good," I would say, "I'm not dating, and I don't need anyone else in my life right now."

Honestly, I was serving the Lord. I was visiting the sick in hospitals, disciplining young women who needed mentorship, and running the youth department. From the youth department to women's ministry, evangelism, and assisting my church and pastor wherever needed. Clearly, you could see that dating was far from my mind.

I loved this season of my life. This is where I really began to learn who I was within. Funny how God will let you go on to a certain point. He was working in my heart the whole time. I just kept going along with my life.

> *"Love is patient and kind; love does not envy or boast; it is not arrogant or rude. It does not insist on its own way, it is not irritable or resentful; it does not rejoice in wrongdoing*

> *but rejoices with the truth. Love bears all things, believes all things, hopes all things, endures all things." 1 Corinthians 13: 4-7*

Love was something I learned to accept over the course of time. Although I had it, I did not know how to effectively show or demonstrate my love to others. I thought I was doing just fine, but I had built a wall around me and resisted receiving love. I was even careful and cautious of how I used the word LOVE.

How could I give what I never had? I associated love with material things. If you did what I liked or wanted you to do for me, that was love.

My first true experience with love was my encounter with the Holy Spirit. The moment I was filled with the Holy Spirit my perspective of love changed. I could not understand how all this love could be given with such grace. I felt unworthy of it, and of course we all are. God's love was unconditional. I did not have to be perfect to receive it. Why me? I've done so many horrible things. I've hurt so many people. How could something so good be given so freely?

That's God's agape love. Period. No strings attached, No conditions, No gimmicks. Just pure unfeigned, untainted, authentic, genuine, agape *love*. When I heard the Holy Spirit speak those three words to me *(I love you)* I literally fell apart. My knees buckled and my heart was so overwhelmed by His presence and gracious love. This was one of the greatest experiences I have ever encountered, and my heart was filled with His liquid *love*.

I felt like I was a new person, like I had never done anything wrong. His presence was so peaceful and joyous at the same time. It felt like I was floating. I was as high as a kite. This was the greatest experience I've ever had in my entire life. It truly transformed the aggressive and violent person I was, into a loving and kind person.

You don't realize how messed up you are until you see your true self in the mirror called life. Although I was a believer, served and loved God with my whole heart, that does not mean that I was perfect. It did not erase the mental trauma I had experienced in life. We usually suppress things until we are challenged in relationships, and we are forced to deal with our issues.

A few months after getting married, I questioned if I had made the right decision. Not because I did not love him, but because I was afraid of what my response would be. I did not want to hurt my husband. He was the most loving, caring, gentle giant I had ever met. He treated me like a queen, and I treated him like a king, but sometimes, every now and then, I would trip like an electric light with a shortage. He would see glimpses of the old me. It would happen sporadically.

One time, I remember spazzing out on my husband and I was embarrassed. Our daughter, who was a toddler, would have temper tantrums where she would fall out. He popped her with his hands on her thighs, telling her to stop. Well, I did not take that too well; the circuit in my mind tripped over into defense mode and I snapped. I went off! I started yelling and crying, saying all kinds of craziness — in front of my daughter, might I add.

I did not blackout as I used to back in the day, so that was a good thing, but I can recall the emotions that rose in me when this happened. For some reason, my mind associated that small thing, when my husband was teaching our daughter to stop throwing tantrums, to something much bigger than that.

I eventually apologized to him for my reaction, but I realized something was not right. I remember having an encounter way before I had gotten married. I was in prayer at my mom's house, and I heard the Holy Spirit tell me, "Yasmine, do you love me?"

I replied, "Lord yes, I do love you."

He said again, "Yasmine, do you love me?"

Again, I said, "Lord, yes, I do love you. Why would you ask me this if you know I do?"

He replied, "Why haven't you given me your whole heart?"

Of course, my reply was, "What do you mean, I have." The moment those words came out of my mouth, it felt like he poked an open wound. I screamed and sobbed like a baby. I quickly jumped out of the prayer because it hurt so bad. I was shocked. I could not believe how long I had carried this pain. I had buried it, not knowing that it would one day surface. I cried out to him asking him to heal my heart.

He replied, "Give it to me. Allow me to heal you by giving me your whole heart." After sobbing, I finally surrendered all to him. My heart was healed that very moment.

I was never challenged in the relationship area to

know whether or not I was totally healed, but I believed I was. My reaction was not a result of me not being healed, because I was. It was a result of me allowing my past to dictate my present and future.

I decided that day I would not allow myself to lose control, because I have self-control. *I can do all things through Christ who strengthens me.* I still have the memory, but it no longer stings or hurts as though it happened yesterday. Why? Because I decided to forgive and let it go completely. How? I allowed the love of God to fill my heart completely.

Forgiveness is what helped me to let go of the experience and replace it with LOVE. Since I forgave, I can LOVE. The greatest feeling one can experience is FREEDOM TO LOVE. Not being held hostage by anything. The word of God says, "Whom the son sets free, is free indeed."

Now I can truly love, and being vulnerable does not bother me because I know I am in a safe place. My heart is not guarded by past experiences anymore. I had to let go of the past to enjoy all the goodness in the present moment.

Let me ask you a question. How are you doing?

Are you free today? Is there an old experience

holding you hostage? Do you feel like you can't be vulnerable because you can't trust anyone? I know where you are, and you are not alone.

You don't have to stay there. God is love and he has given you the liberty to be free. You have your whole life ahead of you. Allow his love to shower your heart by forgiving whomever or whatever it is.

Whatever the circumstance was, you have the power to be free from it by simply forgiving. Forgiving is not for them, they are not held hostage from living their best life, you are. Free yourself today by letting it go.

The moment you open up to let it go, you have opened up to receive that same love God gives freely.

Embrace Forgiveness and Love, that is your portion!

EMBRACING ME

Awakening Your Gift

REFLECTION JOURNALING

Take a notebook and begin writing down what comes to your mind when you ask yourself the following question(s). Be completely honest with yourself.

- Have you received Love?

Part of embracing "YOU" is to love yourself first. Allow God's liquid love to fill your heart. Imagine being an empty pitcher while asking God to fill your heart with his love until your cup overflows. If there is anything in your heart preventing you from walking in perfect love, let it go. You will experience true freedom.

EMBRACING ME

CHAPTER 8
Walking in Soundness

Soundness is having the ability to show good judgment, which results in a calm, well-balanced mind, and self-control. Soundness is then an extension of having a peaceful state of mind.

> *"For God has not given us a spirit of fear, but of power and of love and of a sound mind." 2 Timothy 1:7 NKJ*

In life you will be faced with challenges and situations which will require you to make good decisions. Being sound requires you to be firm and stick to your decisions. When you're sound, you're not easily moved by distractions. You understand you have an assignment, and you stay focused and serve what serves you.

An important part of good judgment is prioritizing, especially when you have deadlines to meet. It enables you to focus on the most important tasks, especially when you know the outcome will be beneficial.

You'll need to learn to trust your judgment, the more you practice it, the better you will become at it. Being sound in your judgment allows you to build character, which is so important to long term success.

You might not realize this, but our words and thoughts have power. Having faith and believing in yourself will determine the outcome of your situation. For instance, if you believe it's going to be a great day; you will indeed have a great day. On the other hand, if you speak negatively and say, "Today is not going to be a good day for me." You will probably have a bad day!

Life can be very unpredictable. Things happened that you have no control over; you do however have control over how you respond. A great example of this was when I hired my first assistant.

After interviewing a potential assistant, I thought she would be a great fit for me and my business. Her strengths were my weakness, she was great at what I sucked at. It seemed like a perfect match.

A few months down the line she had some personal issues which started affecting her at work. I thought this would run its course and everything would go back to normal. That's not the way it happened.

I found myself taking on most of what I had hired her to do. Phone calls and production became very scarce. I knew I had to make an executive decision, but I was afraid to hurt her feelings. I did not want to let her go but when her personal life started affecting her ability to work, I could not afford to keep her.

Once I let her go, it was a huge relief. It gave me peace of mind to know the tasks would get done, instead of hoping she would eventually get the work done. It restored my peace of mind.

Here is another example of things I had no control over. Some of the things I experienced during my childhood years adversely affected me. Of course, I now realize that my mindset and soundness are a byproduct of a firm spiritual foundation. Our soundness comes from the Lord.

According to my mother, she was 6 months pregnant with me when, my parents were in a bad car accident. An eighteen-wheel truck hit the car and sent it spinning into an electric pole. The pole fell on top of the car and totaled it, and somehow my parents crawled out the front window alive. The severity of the accident sent my mom into labor, and she delivered me prematurely at 2lbs 6oz, they weren't sure if I was going to survive.

I lived in the hospital the first precious 3 months of my life. My mom nursed me to health with her tender love and care, along with the support of my dad, a team of nurses, and my doctors.

As I grew up, I remember hearing this story time and time again. I was told I would not be fully competent, that I would have some developmental problems or delays. As a result, I grew up thinking I had limitations. So, in school a "C" was good enough, it was all that could be expected from me.

My favorite subject in school was English. I did well in that subject because I loved it. As an adult I learned, you can set limitations on yourself simply because you don't like something.

I graduated with the *"Thank the Lord, I made it"* mentality. I did it! It was okay because I did not want to stress myself about something I could not control, and I really didn't care about it.

There were many lies the enemy would whisper in my thoughts: *You were a preemie, your mind isn't fully developed, you don't have what it takes, you're dumb, you're not smart, you're slow. You can't keep up with everyone else. That's too hard for you.*

They were all lies! Yes, I may have been a preemie, but the only person that could set those limited beliefs was me.

> *"For the weapons of our warfare are not carnal but mighty through God to the pulling down of strong holds; casting down imaginations, and every high thing that exalts itself against the knowledge of God and bringing into captivity every thought to the obedience of Christ, and having in a readiness to revenge all disobedience, when your obedience is fulfilled." 2 Corinthians 10:4-6*

As I read these scriptures, and meditated on it day and night, my mind began to transform, and grab hold of the TRUTH. The enemy will always take a little fact and intertwine it with lies. The fact that I was born premature did not mean I was dumb or incompetent. That was a LIE! This is why it is imperative to submerge yourself in the word of God, so that your mind can be renewed daily.

Lies are sent to set limited beliefs in your thoughts. Guess what? You do not have to receive them. *Return that junk mail back to the sender.* The enemy, your adversary, will try to plant seeds in your thoughts and have you thinking it's you. You can REBUKE the very thought because all thoughts are not your thoughts. You can boldly stand up and say ABSOLUTELY NOT!

Your mind was not made to be a boxing match for the enemy to torment you. God has given you the power to bring every thought under subjection. You must be firm about what you believe in, so that soundness abides in you. I speak peace so you can embrace soundness of mind. That is your portion.

Now as a business owner, I have another soundness of mind and a different mentality about things. I don't feel the need to know how to do everything, I can hire talented staff. People who add value to my company and compliment my skill set. The more I delegate tasks to another person, the more I can free myself up to do what I really love doing, which is creating, executing, and developing. I can initialize a project and hire people to do what I envisioned.

You don't have to be good at everything, but you should be great at something. When you focus on discovering your greatness and building your own skills, you can excel. Then surround yourself with the right people to come alongside and support you. Developing your skills is what will bring the best out of you. Allowing someone else to do what you're not talented in, is wisdom.

Learning this strategy was the greatest thing that ever happened to me. Now I can walk in my calling and be the best version of myself.

Walking in soundness of mind is a process not a destination. We all fail at times, but as long as we have breath in our body, we always have a second chance and another opportunity to try it again. I've learned, if you're willing, anything is possible.

Awakening Your Gift

REFLECTION JOURNALING

Take a notebook and begin writing down what comes to your mind when you ask yourself the following question(s). Be completely honest with yourself.

- What are some of the limiting beliefs or thoughts that are robbing you of your peace?

EMBRACING ME

Awakening Your Gift

STEP 5: ACCEPTING YOU

EMBRACING ME

CHAPTER 9
Embracing Your Gift

To embrace YOU, you must be willing to receive, accept, and be okay with all of you, not just part of who you are. You can't say I like this about myself, but I don't like that. Why? Because you must be true to yourself. This means loving all of you, including what you believe to be your imperfections.

For years, I thought my dark chocolate skin was an imperfection, so I would bleach it to have a lighter complexion.

The more I sought the Holy Spirit, the more I realized I was perfect in the eyes of God, and the more I loved me. God's love toward me helped me to see that I am a beautiful black Nubian queen. I did not have to bleach my skin because my skin complexion was perfect. This is how God made me, and I now have the boldness to accept it.

When I finally got it, I found something about myself that I loved and highlighted it. I had an outgoing personality, a beautiful smile, and a nice figure. I focused on the good qualities I had.

And eventually I came around accepting my skin complexion and I fell in love with myself as I matured as an adult. I realized that my skin was dark and beautiful. I no longer cared what people said because the way I viewed myself is what mattered.

This truth goes for every aspect of my life. As a result, I carry a different posture. I now speak differently. Even my wardrobe changed when I accepted who I was and who God made me. I have new confidence now. I walk with my head up, shoulders straight and squared, and walk the runway of life.

This transition is when I began to flourish in every aspect of my life. Confidence makes a world of a difference in how you carry yourself and the energy you give off. When you know who you are and *whose* you are, it comes with a level of confidence that you can't hide. It is apparent.

You've been on the potter's wheel, and He has chipped, chiseled, and adjusted, spun you around and placed your feet on solid ground. So now you have a complete makeover. You're happy, you're in a great place mentally, physically, and spiritually. Embrace that, and celebrate the moment because seasons change.

My new confidence helped me step into my purpose; I discovered what God had created me to do.

> *"Just as each one of you has received a special gift (spiritual talent, an ability graciously given by God), employ it in serving one another as {is appropriate for} good stewards of God's multi-faceted grace {faithfully using*

> *the diverse varied gifts and abilities granted to Christians by God's unmerited favor}."* James 4:10

I believe our success is according to our measure of faith. If you believe you're going to make money, you will. If you doubt and say, you're not going to do well, you won't.

God has entrusted each one of us with gifts and it's up to us to use our talents and abilities to multiply them. He knows exactly what you're capable of doing because He created you, and he expects a return on His investment in you. Jesus taught us about this in the Parable of the Talents.

> *"For it is just like a man who was about to take a journey, and he called his servants together and entrusted them with his possessions. To one he gave five talents, to another two, and to another one, each according to his own ability; and then he went on his journey. The one who had received the five talents went at once and traded with them, and he {made a profit and} gained five more. Likewise, the one who had two [made a profit and] gained two more. But the one who had received the one went and dug a hole in the ground and hid his master's*

money.

"Now after a long time the master of those servants returned and settled accounts with them. And the one who had received the five talents came and brought him five more, saying, 'Master, you entrusted to me five talents. See, I have {made a profit and} gained five more talents.' His master said to him, 'Well done, good and faithful servant. You have been faithful and trustworthy over a little, I will put you in charge of many things; share in the joy of your master.'

"Also, the one who had the two talents came forward, saying, 'Master, you entrusted two talents to me. See, I have {made a profit and} gained two more talents.' His master said to him, 'Well done, good and faithful servant. You have been faithful and trustworthy over a little, I will put you in charge of many things; share in the joy of your master.'

"The one who had received one talent also came forward, saying, 'Master, I knew you to be a harsh and demanding man, reaping {the harvest} where you did not sow and gathering where you did not scatter seed. So,

I was afraid {to lose the talent}, and I went and hid your talent in the ground. See, you have what is your own.'

"But his master answered him, 'You wicked, lazy servant, you knew that I reap {the harvest} where I did not sow and gather where I did not scatter seed. Then you ought to have put my money with the bankers, and at my return I would have received my money back with interest. So, take the talent away from him, and give it to the one who has the ten talents.'

"For to everyone who has {and values his blessings and gifts from God, and has used them wisely}, more will be given, and {he will be richly supplied so that} he will have an abundance; but from the one who does not have {because he has ignored or disregarded his blessings and gifts from God}, even what he does have will be taken away. And throw out the worthless servant into the outer darkness; in that place [of grief and torment] there will be weeping [over sorrow and pain] and grinding of teeth {over distress and anger}" Matthew 25: 14-30

I am working the gifts and the talents He has entrusted me with. They were given to me to serve others and not myself.

As you serve, more gifts will be developed. The more you work with what you've got, the more you will multiply. The servant who had five talents doubled to ten. The one who had two doubled to four. It is a proven system that works but you can't be lazy. You must be willing to get out of your comfort zone and employ your gifts, so you can multiply them. If you don't use them, you won't produce anything.

I like to use my garden as an example. When I grow peppers, they produce so many I have to share them, so they won't spoil. I keep a portion for my family, and then distribute the rest to friends, family, and neighbors. If I didn't produce them, I could not provide them for my family or have the ability to bless others with them. The same is true whether it is time, talent, or treasure.

It is also important to understand, to everything, there is a season. Different things are designed for different seasons of our life.

> *"To everything there is a season, and a time to every purpose under the heaven; a time to be born, and a time to die; a time to plant and*

a time to pluck up that which is planted; a time to kill, and a time to heal; a time to break down and a time to build up; a time to weep and a time to laugh; a time to mourn and a time to dance; a time to cast away stones, and a time to gather stones together; a time to embrace and a time to refrain from embracing; a time to get and a time to loose; a time to keep and a time to cast away; a time to rend and a time to sew; a time to keep silence, and a time to speak; a time to love and a time to hate; a time of war and a time of peace." Ecclesiastes 3:1-8

It is time to simply do whatever it is that God brought you on this Earth to do, and what He is calling you to this season in your life. Yes, we have our jobs, careers, and perhaps our own businesses, yet we must still be about His business and be always ready. You have to make yourself available and accessible for whatever it is the Holy Spirit wants to do through and in you.

I embrace all of me because all of me is what God wants me to use. I accept that I have a big mouth to shout aloud with praise and triumph, and victory that will shake loose chains of bondage and set God's people free. I was loud before I surrendered my life to God, and I am even louder now that I have a reason to shout. I shout at the top of my lungs because I know what God delivered me from.

I know I could have been killed when a friend and I foolishly hopped into a drug dealers' vehicle and ended up in a dangerous situation. I cried out to God, "Please save me," and he did. God delivered me.

He spared my life when I lost control of my vehicle on a ramp. My older sister cried, "Jesus stop the car," and the car came to a complete halt. God delivered us.

I know God was with me the day I was contemplating suicide. The enemy was in my ear telling me exactly how to end my life, when a sister from church talked me into going to church instead. God has been good to me.

God wants to use your radicalness because you're not afraid to walk up to someone and tell them that God loves them and has a purpose for their life.

God wants to use your power of prayer, because you don't mind praying for any random person on a dime.

I accept the gift of wisdom, the word of knowledge and prophecy because I tend to yield more to Him in that area and allow him to flow, however, he wants. Well, mostly.

Adjusting to the different seasons of my life has not always been easy. I had to learn to embrace being single for a season. Then I had to adjust to my marriage and becoming a mother. Adjustments to being an employee, being an entrepreneur, serving and ministering to singles and married couples, and for whatever else He needed me for.

At one point in my life, I did not accept every part of me. Before you can be joined with anyone, you yourself must be whole. God comes to make us whole in Him. Meaning you do not need a man or a woman to make you complete; you must be complete entirely in Him. No man wants a woman that is incomplete, and no woman wants a man that is incomplete.

After embracing my single hood, I loved being single. In that season of my life, I got anything I asked God for. He built my confidence in Him; I was confident in me.

I went through a season of wrestling about getting married. I thought to myself, *all this work I've put into bettering myself and all the good times I'm having with just me and the Holy Spirit, I now got to share it*? It was a challenge for me.

God revealed to me that my husband would propose, about a year before it happened. He knew it would take me some time to adjust to the idea. I battled in my mind with how it would work. I was so spoiled and selfish, I could not see me, Him, and the Holy Spirit. What did we need another person in this equation for? We were good!

My emotions were all over the place, I was falling in love, but I did not want to lose control. I don't know what I thought I was controlling but I thought I was okay.

Finally, he proposed to me one day after church service and I was blushing away. I was so happy and nervous at the same time, and I said YES!

Prior to getting married, I heard the Holy Spirit tell me that my life was getting ready to transition. I took it lightly at the time, after all, it's not like we had not had to transition before.

After I had gotten married and the honeymoon was over, it hit me. *Oh my God my routine is changing, I can't come and go as I please*. I had to make some adjustments and, honestly, it was a challenge for me.

I was married but I was still trying to hold on to a

single mentality. I remember my husband asking me one day if I felt like he hindered my ministry, or something along those lines. I was shocked, because that was exactly how I felt but I was not going to confirm it and hurt his feelings, so I said *"No!"* I lied!

This prompted me to go into prayer and seek the Holy Spirit for some help. He reminded me of what he had whispered in my ears prior to me getting married. "This chapter of your life is closing and you're getting ready to transition."

> *"There is a difference between a wife and a virgin. The unmarried woman cares about the things of the Lord, that she may be holy both in body and in spirit. But she who is married cares about the things of the world how she may please her husband." 1 Corinthians 7:34*

My season of being single was over, but I was jealous of the singles. Thankfully, after a few counseling sessions with the Holy Spirit, I was fine. My heart, mind, and spirit were all in agreement and I accepted being a married woman.

I married the love of my life. He was exactly what I needed, and I am so thankful because we are the perfect match. We both love God and the things of God, he's night and I'm day. He's docile, I'm energetic. We are perfect for each other. When I embraced my baby, I saw all the good things we were going to do together as a couple, I was happy.

Transitioning from being a stay-at-home mom to returning to the workforce with kids in daycare was another serious challenge. We had the most beautiful children brought into this world and there was so much joy and adjustment with being a wife and now a mommy.

We are constantly changing and growing, and we make the adjustments necessary to make it work. We have a whole system in place, and it works for our family.

Do what works for you and your family. Don't try to mimic what your friend is doing over at their house, because that may not work with your family dynamics.

We are all here on an assignment and it is timed. We are not here on this Earth forever. One day we will expire here and slip into eternity. While we are here, we must work. Therefore, it is imperative to know who you are and what your assignment is for the season you are in at this moment in time.

Embrace your purpose and do it with your whole

heart as unto God. Everything has a lesson and a purpose. Accept who you are and be willing to make the necessary adjustments to fulfill His purpose for your life.

EMBRACING ME

Awakening Your Gift

REFLECTION JOURNALING

Take a notebook and begin writing down what comes to your mind when you ask yourself the following question(s). Be completely honest with yourself.

- Have you embraced the whole YOU?
- Have you embraced the person God created you to be, with the gifts he has given to you?
- Are you employing your gifts?

EMBRACING ME

CHAPTER 10
Embracing Me

As a child I was very talkative and curious, with a huge imagination. I loved to speak and was always asking *WHY*. If I was told to *not* do something, I wanted to know why! Why wasn't I supposed to talk to strangers? Why wasn't I allowed to cross the street alone or stay out after dark?

These traits have served me well in life. God has used my talents for His own glory and has blessed me beyond measure. I didn't always love who I was, or understand myself, but God knew what He was doing!

We are constantly growing and evolving as we enter new seasons of life, so celebrate your milestones and accomplishments. I encourage you to surrender what does not serve you nor your purpose and embrace the person you were created to be.

> *"Therefore, if anyone is in Christ, the new creation has come: the old has gone, the new is here!"* 2 Corinthians 5:17

I am still learning to keep my priorities right and balance my life: GOD, FAMILY, and BUSINESS. Life will happen, and things may not always go as planned. It's okay. It's up to us how we choose to handle every situation. If we keep God as the main thing in our life, there will always be victories.

Embracing myself started when I was able to accept my identity **(Step 1)**. When I accepted myself, I learned to love who I was becoming and became excited about where I was going. Now, I am excited about the journey.

Looking back, I can see how much I have grown, matured, and blossomed as a woman. Being willing to do the work is what really changed my life. I can honestly say the Holy Spirit is indeed a helper and a leader, and He guides me in everything I do. I take no credit.

It took time to discover who God created me to be, and even longer to accept it. Your journey will look different than mine, but it will be a process for you as well.

My journey of discovery started as I spent time seeking my creator. I turned to the Bible, the owner's manual **(Step 2)** for this life. This is where I learned that I had indeed been created with a purpose. It was up to me to pray and believe and awaken that purpose within me.

"The purpose in a man's heart is like deep water, but a man of understanding will draw it out." Proverbs 20:5

There is work required to draw it out, you must be willing to seek, ask, and knock. You must inquire and be relentless about obtaining an answer. Seeking God in prayer. Have a spirit of expectation and begin thanking God for answering your prayers.

Ask God to make you more aware of your surroundings. Your answers may not come packaged the way you expect, be careful not to miss an opportunity.

Now looking back, I realize that my dad was an entrepreneur. He never worked a regular 9-5 job, as a matter of fact, I use to go with him on some of his projects. He had clients everywhere and did pretty much everything from plumbing, roofing, and carpentry to auto repair. No doubt he ignited the entrepreneur in me.

My mom was not really a fan of the entrepreneurial path, she believed in consistency and security. She said, "As long as you go to work, you know you will get a paycheck." Trading my time for pay was okay, it paid most of my bills. But as I grew older, I knew I wanted to take a different approach to earn my money, I wanted to become an entrepreneur.

This was no surprise to God! The more I stepped into my calling and purpose, the more my desire to become an entrepreneur grew. I knew it would free up my time to do what I love, which is being creative.

I didn't just abruptly leave my job, my husband and I talked about it and planned for the day I could take that leap of faith and leave my 9 to 5 job. Thankfully, my husband is very supportive, which means so much to me. We understood the risks and were willing to take a chance.

I started creating what I envisioned. I saw myself being my own boss, while creating opportunities for others. I could see the need for a service that would fulfill my calling to help, encourage, empower, and equip women to be the best version of themselves.

As crazy as this sounds, and I'm sure every entrepreneur can attest to this as well, being an entrepreneur is not as easy as it looks. Yes, I love the freedom of being my own boss, but *it also comes with a greater responsibility.*

I find myself working longer hours, burning the midnight oil if you will, and waking up an hour earlier so I can get more out of the day. The first to wake up and the last to go to bed. I have never worked so hard, as I have for myself. Yet, It's gratifying.

Often, as a new entrepreneur you must wear multiple hats, working several positions. Since, I was not financially ready to hire any extra help, I had to work twice as hard. This gave me the opportunity to learn about my own strengths and gifts, and it gave me insights into what I should hire someone else to do! Just because I can do somethings does not mean I will have the capacity to be consistent.

One of the gifts I discovered I had was the gift of exhortation. Encouraging, motivating, and empowering people to do what they are called to do, comes easy for me.

Yes, I am an exhorter. I love to empower, encourage, and build people up to be the best version of themselves, while exercising their faith. I simply love helping people. I was created to serve others.

I am passionate about seeing women fulfill their purpose, and I have had the privilege of seeing many women doing that. It fills my heart with joy. When I finally accepted what my calling was, my purpose was clearly defined, and *Awakening Your Gift* was birthed.

Once I embraced my calling and had a clear vision for the future, it was time to hit the reset button **(Step 3)** and transform my mind. Learning about it is one thing, but applying it is a process. I renewed my mind daily by reading my Bible and connecting with likeminded people.

I also had to separate myself from those who were NOT likeminded, I could not afford to revert to my old way of doing things. Changing the people, I interacted with, was conducive to my growth and goal. I thought differently. I acted differently. I even moved differently.

I surrounded myself with wise counsel. People who had accomplished what I was trying to achieve. People who knew more than I did. Transformation took place when I became serious about changing and becoming a better version of who God created me to be.

If you want to get different results, you must be willing to do something different. Something that is going to get you closer to your objectives and goals.

Find someone you admire or look up to, perhaps a Leader or Pastor. If you need one, hire a coach or mentor. Find someone to hold you accountable. It is very easy to lose focus and become discouraged in this process. You must have the right person in your ear. Not your cousin, aunt, uncle, or friend who has never stepped out of their comfort zone to accomplish anything.

Surround yourself with a community of like-minded individuals, so you can feed off each other and grow. They will help you stay away from the dream killers.

The greatest experience of the transformation process came when I discovered the liberty **(Step 4)** God gives us. When I stepped into who God created me to be, I was suddenly free to be, unapologetically me! I found a sense of belonging and purpose. I no long worry if a person likes me or if they accept me for who I am.

Why? Because I am walking in power, love, and soundness!

God gave us authority over all things. Fear no longer controls me because my love is perfect. I trust that God has me and He is in control of everything.

This soundness comes from having the peace of God that surpasses all understanding. I've learned that anything that is beyond my control is not my problem. Your peace is your assurance. You don't need to entertain every thought. Do not allow what's happening on the outside to disturb your inner peace. If it's beyond your control, hand it over to the one who is greater than you.

Seasons in your life will change, and you will need to adjust. When you embrace the process and where you are, you can accept this will pass. These times may not feel great in the moment, but if you're flowing in the same direction with the current, you can rest in Him. It will get better.

The best thing you can do for yourself is to accept who you are **(Step 5)** and embrace who God created YOU to be. Who you are called to serve. The more you use your gifts, the more you will discover about yourself.

Every time you use it you are developing that muscle and becoming stronger. After a while, you will discover something else and master that. It's the gift that keeps on giving.

> "But unto every one of us is given grace according to the measure of the gift of Christ." Ephesians 4:7

The more you serve, the greater your capacity

becomes, and the more He will entrust you with. Life is not about what you can get or receive. It's about what you do with what you have. It's about what you can give. How you can impact the lives of others and make a difference by adding value to someone else.

The gift God has given to you is precious and priceless. When you find what it is, embrace it. Your Gift will make room for you. He will clear the pathway for you and lead you to places you could have never thought or imagined.

Your Gift will lead you to greatness. When you awaken the gift and purpose God has called you to, you will find fulfillment in life.

Embracing who you are is about accepting your calling or purpose. My prayer is that this book will be a tool to help you take the steps towards discovering who God created you to be. The steps that will lead you to your divine purpose.

> *"But seek ye first the kingdom of God and His righteousness; and all these things shall be added to you."* Matthew 6:33

My heart's desire is to fulfill God's purpose to the highest expectation. When I leave this earth, I want to leave empty and not full. My mission, and my desire, is to serve you at my fullest potential with the gift He has freely given to me.

Awakening Your Gift is a movement. I'm on a mission to do what fulfills me and edifies others. Seeing people embracing their gifts fulfills my purpose. I am passionate about what He's called me to do, and I understand the assignment.

My prayer is that you will live to the highest calling God has called you to and serve in the spirit of gratitude and excellence.

"Get up and Go Get It."

Awakening Your Gift

REFLECTION JOURNALING

Take a notebook and begin writing down what comes to your mind when you ask yourself the following question(s). Be completely honest with yourself.

- What do you see yourself doing effortlessly?
- What is your purpose?
- Who were you called to serve?

You may need a coach or a mentor to help cultivate that special, unique gift that was given to you. Embrace it and you will blossom into the beautiful flower that will make a difference in serving others.

… EMBRACING ME

ABOUT THE AUTHOR

The 4th child of 10 siblings, Yasmine Brown gained her first leadership skills as a big sister.

Yasmine is an innately enthusiastic exhorter. She loves to encourage, empower, and impact the people she meets, by challenging them to be the best version of themselves.

She also inspires them to dream big, building their confidence while embracing their unique gifts and capabilities. She has turned her stories into teaching tools; catapulting people to success through small steps that produce massive results.

Amongst all her creative business endeavors, she is a licensed realtor in the state of Florida and has recently become a real estate investor with the Women's Real Estate Investors Network. She vlogs @YasRealHomes on YouTube about her profession as a passionate real estate agent serving her community. She uses her experience as an expert in her field, to help serve her client's real estate needs.

Yasmine Brown is also an active member at The River Church at Ft. Myers, Florida. It's no wonder she heads up the Kingdom Business Department, teaching people practical business steps using kingdom principles. She also helps serve with other ministries when needed.

Yasmine Brown is also a philanthropist, and has partnered with the Youth Impact Outreach Organization, helping children in Haiti to have a better quality of living through education. Yasmine Brown LLC donates a portion of every house sold to Youth Impact Organization.

https://yasrealhomes.com/content/youth-impact-outreach.

Yasmine has been married for 18 years to her best friend, Fabian, and lives in Florida with her husband and 2 beautiful children.

To learn more visit: www.awakeningyourgift.com

Made in the USA
Columbia, SC
07 February 2023